Also by Wyn Beasley

HISTORY AND BIOGRAPHY

FELLOWSHIP OF THREE (1993)
The lives and association of John Hunter, James Cook and Joseph Banks

PORTRAITS AT THE ROYAL AUSTRALASIAN COLLEGE
OF SURGEONS (1993)

HOME AWAY FROM HOME (2000)

IN BLACK AND WHITE (2008)
A short memoir of Jim & Emmy Bellwood

INSTITUTIONAL HISTORY

THE LIGHT ACCEPTED (1992)
125 years of Wellington College

BORNE FREE (1995)
The Wellington Free Ambulance 1927-1994

THE CLUB ON THE TERRACE (1996)
The Wellington Club 1841-1996

THE MANTLE OF SURGERY (2002)
The first 75 years of the Royal Australasian College of Surgeons

CHURCHILL
THE SUPREME SURVIVOR

The 1941 photographic portrait of Winston Churchill by Karsh of Ottawa became instantly famous because it captured so perfectly Churchill's refusal to be defeated by the menace that faced his country, and indeed the civilised world. Back in June 1940 he had proclaimed: 'We shall never surrender.' In confronting a wide variety of medical adventures he displayed a similar attitude to misfortune.

CHURCHILL
THE SUPREME SURVIVOR

A.W. BEASLEY

First published in 2013 by Mercer Books
www.mercerbooks.co.uk

ISBN 978-0-9557127-3-9

A CIP catalogue record for this book is available from The British Library

Design by Reuben Wakeman
Printed in the UK by Butler Tanner & Dennis, Frome

For Martin Gilbert

il miglior fabbro

CONTENTS

FOREWORD

by General Sir Peter de la Billière KCB KBE DSO MC MSC DL

As a Harrow schoolboy in the late 1940s, I recall a series of visits to the school by its most famous Old Boy, Winston Churchill. He had been Britain's wartime leader, but had been bundled out of office in 1945 and was now Leader of the Opposition. I can recall the rapturous applause he received, with much cheering and waving, and then we all went mad and followed him into the street outside the Headmaster's House to continue our noisy appreciation. It is so clear in my mind that I almost feel I met him.

It pleases me, therefore, that my friend Wyn Beasley has set about documenting the enormous and varied array of medical adventures, many of them life-threatening, that beset Churchill during his long life, and I find myself speculating on what might have been the course of history if Sir Winston had not been the supreme survivor that he was. It also pleases me that Wyn has been able to explain so many of these conditions in language that is easy for the layman to follow, and describe the management of various disorders in the pre-antibiotic days in which Sir Winston lived most of his life.

From 1940 onwards, Churchill was cared for, loyally and at some sacrifice, by Sir Charles McMoran Wilson, who became his personal physician at the urging of his Cabinet when he succeeded to the post of Prime Minister of a seemingly doomed Great Britain. In 1943 Wilson became Lord Moran, and two years later he published a small book, *The anatomy of courage*, based on his experience as a front-line medical officer in the 1914-18 War, where he was awarded a Military Cross. This book became a recognised military text, and when I wrote my study of a number of Victoria Cross recipients, *Supreme Courage*, almost a decade ago, Moran's book helped me a great deal in understanding the basis of their deeds. It was a privilege, therefore, to provide a foreword for the re-issue of *The anatomy of courage* shortly afterwards.

There is an irony in the fact that, in writing this present foreword, I am subscribing to a warts-and-all assessment of Lord Moran and his treatment of Churchill. Wyn Beasley has examined a number of 'Churchill myths' and in some cases has traced them to the public interpretation of comments made by Lord Moran when he published what has been called 'a vast and highly readable tome of reminiscences of his relations' with Churchill. Such myths have proved remarkably durable, and have caused Churchill to be labelled, among other faults, as a depressive and a heavy drinker; neither quality is consistent with his performance as Britain's wartime prime minister.

It is good that we have this new contribution to the Churchill record, and at a time when attention is once again being directed to the man who has been recognised as 'the greatest Englishman of the twentieth century' it is refreshing to have an account of him that breaks new ground, and provides a perspective that perhaps only a surgeon could offer.

Peter de la Billière

INTRODUCTION

This story has been a long time in the making. As a schoolboy during the Second World War, I used to be wakened during the night on numerous occasions to listen to one of Churchill's wartime speeches. My father (who had served in the First War) had long been an admirer of Churchill, and was repeatedly furious with the political midgets who failed to respond to his warnings.

Now this was not simply prejudice against the Germans (he had often contrasted French squalor with German tidiness, as gauged during his war and immediately afterwards when he was part of the original Army of Occupation) – but he summed up Nazism sooner than many, and he felt an affinity with Churchill during the Wilderness (or Locust) Years, which was reinforced during the War itself.

Over the next half-century, I retained my childhood respect for Churchill. I felt some embarrassment when he held on as Prime Minister, as it seemed, past his use-by date; but I rejoiced at the serendipity of my first visit to the House of Commons, which coincided with his final speech as PM. I recognised that Britain had 'traded down' when I heard Eden speak on our street corner in Eltham in the 1955 election campaign because, some years before Peter Sellars recorded his classic 'Party Political Speech', I heard it delivered, that day at the corner of our street.

I cringed again later, when Lord Moran broke the rules of patient confidentiality, but what I had heard of him made it all seem rather in character. He was a somewhat controversial figure as president of the Royal College of Physicians of London, who had been 'wished' on Churchill as personal physician, when the Cabinet decided (after Churchill became Prime Minister in May 1940) that such an appointment was desirable. He was Sir Charles McMoran Wilson then; he was ennobled in 1943; and within months of Churchill's death he published his 'diaries' under the sub-title *The struggle for survival*, giving his account of how he had kept a derelict premier alive.

In 1973 I was fortunate enough to be awarded a Winston Churchill Memorial Fellowship, which enabled me to travel widely and study the subject of 'research and education in the field of road safety'. This sharpened up my loyalty to the ideas of Churchill (and Empire!) on which I had been brought up – at least until an immigration clerk at Heathrow looked down his nose and asked: 'Whaiy are you heah?'… I followed the progress of posthumous biography which built on the volumes (Hugh Martin, Philip Guedalla, Lewis Broad, later Alan Moorehead) that I had read in my youth; but I followed it casually, and with some doubt about Randolph's ability, as official biographer, to do justice to his father (though, having since read his own two volumes, I am reassured).

Then Martin Gilbert's fascinating detective story *In search of Churchill* came out, and I was encouraged by the thought that now, certainly, my hero's story was in safe hands. And when the Folio Society's two volume edition of Gilbert's *Churchill: a life* arrived, I realised that here (quite apart from its quality as the record of a great life) was a treasure in terms of the raw material of medical history. Allen Packwood has written: 'Sir Martin's brilliant and monumental works constitute the starting point for all serious study of Winston Churchill', and I can only confirm and applaud that judgment.

As I began to string together an account of Churchill's quite extraordinary medical odyssey, I found family and friends offering me copies of other recent biographies: those of Geoffrey Best and Roy Jenkins in particular proved valuable - even if Jenkins did seem intent at times on proving how far Churchill's career had emulated his own. It became evident from these accounts that, if Churchill had been a cat, he would have used up his nine lives during – if not well before – his nine decades. He himself admitted to being a risk-taker, but medical adventures of one sort or another seemed to pursue him from his very birth.

An opportunity to present the story for the first time came in mid-2005. Churchill had become an honorary Fellow of the Royal College of Surgeons of England in 1943, and at the twice-yearly diplomates' day of the College, an open lecture is accommodated in what would otherwise be an awkward hiatus between the ceremony, and the College dinner that follows in the evening. I had discharged the lecture requirements of my Hunterian Professorship in this time slot in 2002, and had enjoyed the occasion.

This time it was agreed that the medical history of an illustrious honorary Fellow would be an appropriate topic and that I might therefore be trusted with another chance – the material was judged of general enough interest to appeal to an audience largely made up of euphoric diplomates and proud parents. It was once again a rewarding experience; but this time I was deluged with additional information, contacts opened up, and what had hitherto been a mild exercise in curiosity came to resemble a crusade.

It was a crusade that involved me in my first detailed examination of Moran's book, of which hitherto I had read only a condensed version. That experience had been trying enough, and frequently irritating because of the rather patronising style of Moran's recollections; but the task of working through the whole eight hundred pages of smallish type in the original produced a disturbing sense of betrayal, which re-reading has done nothing to dispel – not just Moran's betrayal of the confidence that his patient had placed in him, but the way in which Moran had succeeded in betraying his own meanness of spirit (and, in places, what struck me as his underlying inadequacies). I wondered, for instance, why he got to Carthage without arming himself with a supply of digitalis, and had to 'send to Tunis' for it when Churchill went into atrial fibrillation; I wondered how he could gloss over so much of his patient's history (of which he ought to have been aware) as to assert that, even in 1943, Churchill had little experience of serious ailments; and I wondered about the professional standards of a president of the College of Physicians who 'demolished the President of the other College [i.e. the College of Surgeons] in *The Times* without any mercy' – for this is what he proudly quotes Churchill as saying about him in one of the dialogues he records. (I am not aware that the surgical president concerned, Sir Alfred, later Lord, Webb-Johnson was in need of demolition, by Moran or anyone else.)

Most of all I wondered how Churchill could continue to function as the war leader he was, in the face of the dosage of barbiturates with which Moran used to treat him. It is common experience that older people, especially those in retirement homes, prosper quite often when their therapeutic menu is reviewed and trimmed. A recent film, *Mrs Caldicot's Cabbage War*, built very successfully on this phenomenon. I am prompted to wonder if Churchill needed a Mrs Caldicot more than a Lord Moran at times.

I am grateful to all those who have contributed to the deluge of information that I mentioned earlier. I should single out the Director, Mr Allen Packwood and his staff at the Churchill Archives Centre at Churchill College, Cambridge, without whom this undertaking would have been left seriously incomplete; and I must also offer special thanks to Lady Soames for her willingness to have me run my assumptions past her, to Sir Peter de la Billière for having agreed to contribute a foreword to the work he had already done so much to facilitate, and to Sir Martin Gilbert for his generous and expert counsel, which I have acknowledged in a phrase borrowed from T S Eliot. I am grateful to Mr Bernard (now Lord) Ribeiro for the invitation, to speak at his College in 2005, that catalysed the project. Others to whom I owe a debt of gratitude include my medical sons, Spencer and Richard, who have cast an eye over my medical opinions – if these opinions are sound, they have probably contributed; if not, they should be considered blameless. I would also thank Prof René Baumgartner, Lady de la Billière, Dr J Hugh Baron, Mr Ross D Blair, Dr Michael C Brain, Prof Timothy W R Briggs, the late Sir Anthony Montague Browne, Dr Bruce Cook, Mr Peter Devane, Dr Ronald Easthope, Mr Peter A Fabian, Dr Gillon Ferguson, Dr Susan and the late Mr Geoffrey Fisk, Mr Nigel Guest, the late Mr Godfrey How, Prof Kaye Ibbertson, Sir Barry Jackson, Prof Keith Jeffery, Mr Iain M C Macintyre, Mr Iain MacLaren, Mr John McLean, Prof Sam Mellick, Dr William Patterson, Prof Donald Simpson, Miss Valerie Steele, Prof Alan Thurston, the Lord Turnberg, the late Prof Jeffray Weston, the late Sir John White, Mr Anthony J K Woodhead, who have contributed in various ways; and the many people who have shown interest in the work and have provided encouragement. My visit to Cambridge in mid-2006 was undertaken with the aid of a research grant from Wakefield Health, Wellington, and to that forward-looking institution I express my appreciation. I am once again indebted to the Medical Research Institute of New Zealand for administrative support. During the publishing process I have come to appreciate the skill and helpfulness of Tim Mercer and Reuben Wakeman at Mercer Books. My wife's support of my literary endeavours is now well into its third decade: what more can I say about such loyalty.

Although Churchill's adventures spanned so many branches of medicine and are therefore of wide medical interest – they include cardiology, respiratory medicine, neurology, general surgery and orthopaedics, to name but a few – I have tried to give an account of them in terms that the lay reader can readily appreciate. I am reminded of the words of one of my old chiefs, warning against the overuse of jargon: there are only two technical terms in medicine, he pointed out, that cannot be rendered in simpler language – and they are 'left' and right'.

WYN BEASLEY
Wellington, New Zealand

I

ALL VERY TIRESOME

We toiled each day…
I thought it all very tiresome.

- WSC: *My early life,* ch. 1

Winston Leonard Spencer Churchill was born on 30 November 1874. He was the first child of Lord Randolph Churchill – a younger son of the 7th Duke of Marlborough – and Jeanette [Jennie], the daughter of Leonard Jerome.

Jerome was a colourful figure, an American financier and newspaper king who was also one of the founding figures of American horseracing, a buccaneer who made and lost fortunes and fascinated women (even his own longsuffering wife). The young couple had met at Cowes in the summer of 1873, fallen promptly in love, and succeeded in overcoming parental reservations (on both sides) so as to be married in Paris on 15 April the following year.

1 Winston was the son of Lord Randolph Churchill and Jennie, daughter of the American entrepreneur Leonard Jerome.

The announcement in *The Times* labelled the birth as premature. This wording used to be a diplomatic means of indicating that the young couple had 'jumped the gun'; but various biographers attest to a genuinely premature birth – Moorehead says the child arrived 'a full six weeks before he was expected'[1] and Churchill's official biographer Martin Gilbert records that Lady Randolph 'then less than seven months pregnant' had slipped and fallen while walking with a shooting party at Blenheim Palace;[2] and had gone into labour while riding in a pony carriage over rough ground a few days later. It was a somewhat precipitate onset, and she had time only to get back to Blenheim and deliver her son in a small cloakroom near the entrance.

The whole business found the Blenheim establishment unprepared: Lady Randolph's pains began on Saturday night, persisted through Sunday, and her child was delivered at 1.30a.m. on the Monday. Attempts to contact the Oxford physician were fruitless, as was a telegraphic summons to her obstetrician Dr Hope in London – Sunday was Sunday in those days – but, as Lord Randolph wrote to his mother-in-law later on Monday morning, 'the country Dr is however a clever man'. The child, he reported, was 'very healthy considering his prematureness [*sic*]'; and in a postscript he documented the household's principal difficulty: 'I hope the baby things will come with all speed. We had to borrow some from the Woodstock solicitor's wife.'

The Duchess of Marlborough, writing to her new co-grandmother that day, (Mrs Jerome was then, indeed mostly, resident in Paris) enlarged on the deficiencies: 'We had neither cradle nor baby linen nor anything ready'; but four days later she could report that 'the little boy is a very healthy pretty little child, and I think will be a large Child in time.'[3] I think the business of Winston's prematurity must be taken as factual rather than diplomatic. Unfortunately the Blenheim unpreparedness extended to matters such as recording the infant's birth weight, it seems; but the delay in young Winston's baptism, until 27 December (in the Blenheim chapel) argues a tiny baby who needed several weeks to mature – yet whose survival was never despaired of.

* * *

Then, and indeed for many years afterwards, premature birth carried a serious mortality. Neonatal units for premature babies had yet to be thought of. As recently as 1950, Professor Alan Moncrieff began an essay on the management of the premature baby with these words: 'According to official figures twice as many premature infants die each year in Great Britain as the total number of all persons killed on the roads. Half of these deaths occur in the first 24 hours of life and present a challenge to the obstetrician to prevent premature labour, but better management of the survivors would go far to reduce the loss of life.'[4]

Moncrieff's advice on management was given in respect of 'a group of infants whose weights ranged from 2 lb. (1kg.) or less up to the official standard of 5½ lb. (2.5 kg.)' – he was dealing with infants rather less premature than the extreme survivors of today, and describing a sample more typical of Churchill's day. That is to say, Churchill's prospects of survival at birth, like those of the babies in Moncrieff's series, were indifferent, at best. But he did survive.

* * *

Young Winston went through the aristocratic sequence of a governess, then boarding at a preparatory school. His parents were therefore somewhat remote figures, his mother a glittering part of Victorian society, his father an up-and-coming politician. Lord Randolph had entered Parliament in the year of Winston's birth, and had impressed Disraeli the Prime Minister with his maiden speech: 'The House was surprised, and then captivated, by his energy, and natural flow, and his impressive manner. With self-control and study, he might mount. It was a speech of great promise.' (But self-control was not one of Lord Randolph's qualities.) The following year, as Winston later observed in his biography of his father,

Lord and Lady Randolph Churchill installed themselves in a large house in Charles Street, where they continued their gay life on a somewhat more generous scale than their income warranted.[5]

When the Duke of Marlborough was appointed Lord-Lieutenant of Ireland in 1876, Lord Randolph accompanied him as his secretary – as his honorary secretary, of course. Young Winston's earliest memories were therefore of being a small but observant part of Dublin society. 'My mother,' Winston would write, (endorsing Lord D'Abernon's account of Lady Randolph's appearance – 'a dark, lithe figure… radiant, translucent, intense' - at the Vice-Regal Lodge in Dublin), 'made the same brilliant impression upon my childhood's eye. She shone for me like the Evening

Star. I loved her dearly – but at a distance. My nurse was my confidante. Mrs Everest it was who looked after me and tended all my wants. It was to her I poured out all my troubles, both now and in my schooldays.'[6]

At school he experienced the rigours of educational sadism. In his autobiography, *My Early Life*, he recorded how:

> **...delinquents were haled off to an adjoining apartment by the two head boys, and there flogged until they bled freely, while the rest sat quaking, listening to their screams. This form of correction was strongly reinforced by frequent religious services of a somewhat High Church character in the chapel... I... did not derive much comfort from the spiritual side of my education at this juncture. On the other hand I experienced the fullest applications of the secular arm.[6]**

Well, gluteal [that is to say, of the buttocks] lacerations heal; but what other effects (and how durable) did such rituals achieve?

His report for the spring term of 1884 makes it plain that the school, while well enough aware of his potential, was quite unable to make an impression on the boy: his teacher, H Martin Cooke, complained 'conduct has been exceedingly bad. He is not to be trusted to do any one thing. He has however notwithstanding made decided progress'; and the headmaster concurred: 'Very bad – is a constant trouble to everybody and is always in some scrape or other. He cannot be trusted to behave himself anywhere.' And then, grudgingly, 'He has very good abilities. H W Sneyd Kynnersley.' Now the challenge of capturing the interest of a bright badly-behaved (which usually means 'bored') child is one that ought to bring out the best in a school or a teacher: plainly St George's School, Ascot, and Messrs Kynnersley and Cooke, failed to meet the challenge.

Certainly Churchill himself recorded that he 'fell into a low state of health at St James's school [his error with the name is probably significant]

> **and finally after a serious illness my parents took me away. Our family doctor, the celebrated Robson Roose, then practised at Brighton; and as I was now supposed to be very delicate, it was thought desirable that I should be under his constant care. I was accordingly, in 1883, transferred to a school at Brighton kept by two ladies'.[6]**

Here he found 'an element of kindness and of sympathy… conspicuously lacking in my first experiences', but was overtaken by two misfortunes: an argument with another boy (recorded by Gilbert) which caused young Winston – then barely 10 – to be stabbed in the chest with a penknife; and 'an attack of double pneumonia' which he himself described. His father had written, from the South of France, to his wife at the beginning of 1883:

> **I'm sorry poor little Winston has not been well, but I don't make out what is the matter with him. It seems we are a sickly family and cannot get rid of the doctors.'**

It is probably not overstating matters to propose absentee parenting as one of the boy's disabilities.

Another, long veiled in obscurity, was the development of a hernia, concerning which he made no mention until 1945, when it troubled him afresh. But then, in a letter to his wife, he confided:

> **Darling a tiresome thing has happened to me. When I was v[er]y young I ruptured myself & had to wear a truss. I left it off before I went to Harrow.**[7]

In those days the use of a truss to control the bulging of a hernia was orthodox management; in 1895 the surgeon Frederick Treves (who will appear later in this story) claimed that it offered a 15-20 per cent chance of curing the condition.[8] This it may even have achieved, in the medium term, for Winston.

It is not surprising that the truss was discarded before young Winston began at Harrow. Even a less sensitive child would have hesitated to appear at boarding school thus encumbered; but from the fact that he started at Harrow at the age of 13, in early 1888, I think it is reasonable to regard the original development of his hernia as an event of his first decade. Its later effects on him will emerge in due course.

Table 1

THE FIRST DECADE 1874-84

Premature birth

Gluteal lacerations (corporal punishment)

Chest laceration (pocketknife wound)

Pneumonia

Hernia

NOTES

1   Moorehead, A: *Churchill – a pictorial Biography*. 1960; London: Thames & Hudson. p.10.

2   Gilbert, M: *Churchill – a life*. 2004; London: Folio Society. [Originally published 1991; London: Heinemann.] p.1.

3   These items of correspondence are printed in *Companion Volume 1, part 1*, of Randolph Churchill's edition of his father's papers [London: Heinemann, 1967: p.1 ff]. Lord Randolph's letter was posted for him by Dr Hope, who had arrived on the Monday morning to find that Dr Frederic Taylor (physician and surgeon to the Woodstock police, and coroner for Woodstock) had everything under control. The solicitor's wife who had come to the rescue with new-baby apparatus was herself delivered of a son on 28 January 1875.

4   Moncrieff, A: Management of the Premature Baby; in *Refresher Course for General Practitioners I*. 1952; London, BMA: p.27

5   Churchill, W S: *Lord Randolph Churchill*. London, 1906. p.61 in the Odhams edition. Churchill's attitude to the relation between money and show becomes easy to appreciate.

6   Churchill, W.S: *My Early Life*. 1944; London: Reprint Society. [originally published 1930; London: Macmillan] pp. 13, 20, 21. His transfer to Brighton took place in September 1884.

7   Soames, M: *Clementine Churchill: the revised and updated biography*. 2002; London: Doubleday. p. 433.

8   Treves, F. *A system of Surgery*. 1895: II: 680.

II

HARROW

I enjoyed the Harrow songs…[1]
There is certainly nothing
like them at Eton.

- WSC: *My early life,* ch. 3.

I n March 1886 the doctors were on the scene again, when Winston, aged 11, came close to death with another attack of pneumonia. Dr Roose wrote to Sir Randolph:

> **I am in the next room, and shall watch the patient during the night – for I am anxious… I used stimulants, by the mouth and rectum, with the result that [the temperature fell from 104 to 101].**

Three days later he could report that

> **Winston has had six hours quiet sleep. Delirium has now ceased. Temp 99, P 92, R 28.**[2]

* * *

It is not easy, in these antibiotic days, to appreciate what a killer pneumonia used to be, or how dramatic was its clinical course. Even the terminology was dramatic – 'the crisis' was a term to be employed in whispers lest its effect become overwhelming. In 1912 Herbert French, physician to Guy's Hospital, wrote of a typical history, 'the sudden onset of an acute pulmonary complaint associated with fine crepitations [crackling sounds heard through the stethoscope] confined to one or more lobes, followed by dullness [loss of the normal resonance on tapping the chest]… Viscid, rusty sputum is almost pathognomonic [diagnostic] of pneumonia.'[3]

The typical infecting organism was the pneumococcus: this entered the air-sacs or alveoli in the finest subdivisions of the branching system of tubes in the lung. It generally affected one part of this system, that is to say, one lobe of a lung (but on occasions could involve several lobes or even a part of each lung; 'double pneumonia' enjoyed a particularly evil reputation). It produced an outpouring of sticky fluid to turn the affected lobe into a block of tissue resembling raw liver in consistency. Not surprisingly, this process was termed 'hepatisation' and two stages were identified in the post-mortem specimens that resulted not uncommonly from such a disease: red and grey hepatisation.

So far as the patient was concerned, a high fever would persist for several days, with delirium common, and oxygenation of the blood seriously compromised. It will have been noted that Dr Roose used 'stimulants by mouth and rectum': of strychnine it was written as late as 1952 that 'the most important use of strychnine is as a respiratory stimulant'[4] and, although by then the drug was employed mainly in the treatment of poisoning by respiratory depressants, it would have been Roose's drug of choice, probably in the form known as 'nux vomica'.

French describes the progress of the fever: 'The patient's temperature, after maintaining a high level such as 103°F or 104°F [39.5-40°C] for from five to ten days – usually about seven – falls by crisis [which is here an heroic term for 'abruptly']. The respiration rate is very rapid – for example, 40 per minute – during the height of the fever, and the skin is flushed, dry, pungent before the crisis, moist from profuse perspiration after it.'[3] Because there was no specific treatment and only the combination of nursing measures and dubious prescribing was available, it was a trying and exhausting time for doctor, relatives and patient alike – with the qualification in this case that young Winston's parents were typically absent. Dr Roose's sojourn at the bedside is easy to understand; his relief once the crisis had passed would have been shared by Winston himself.

But it was July before the boy could return to school.

* * *

2 Lord Randolph Churchill as Chancellor of the Exchequer, 1886. This post, briefly held, was the summit of Lord Randolph's political career. To emulate his father would become Winston's ambition.

Meanwhile his father's Conservative party had won a general election and Lord Randolph became Chancellor of the Exchequer – though not for long, because he offered his resignation on a point of principle (a tactic he had previously employed successfully) and on this occasion, even before he had presented a Budget, his resignation was accepted.

To emulate his father's success would become one of the boy's great ambitions (to emulate his father's political vicissitudes would be the price he would pay). First, though, this recalcitrant child had an education to complete.

3 The boy was sent to Harrow-on-the-Hill on account of his presumed fragile health, after a couple of episodes of pneumonia during his early years.

Because of his earlier ill-health his parents opted not for Eton, his father's school, but for Harrow-on-the-Hill. His career there was mixed: he languished in the lower forms, while winning a prize for committing 1000 lines of Macaulay's *Lays of Ancient Rome* to memory. And he won the Public Schools fencing competition. At 14 he joined the 'Army Class' in preparation for Sandhurst.

But Harrow found as much difficulty in coping

with Winston's behaviour as had St George's, Ascot. A letter dated 12th July 1888, written to his mother by the assistant master, Henry Davidson, reads:

Dear Lady Randolph Churchill
    After a good deal of
hesitation and discussion with
his form-master, I have decided
to allow Winston to have his
exeat: but I must own that
he has not deserved it. I do
not think, nor does Mr Somervell,
that he is in any way <u>wilfully</u>
troublesome: but his forgetfulness,
carelessness, unpunctuality, and
irregularity in every way, have
really been so serious, that I
write to ask you, when he is
at home, to speak very gravely
to him on the subject.

However, Lady Randolph was seldom at home when her son was; nor did her social life allow her to visit her son as often as he hoped.

That Christmas, home on holiday, he reported in a letter to his mother (who was herself away travelling) that his throat was 'painful & swelled' and his liver 'bad'. Back at school he fell off his bicycle and was in bed for a week with concussion. His mother was conspicuous by her absence: 'I was rather disappointed at not seeing you as I fully expected to,' he wrote. And then his teeth started to give trouble. The correspondence between young Winston, his parents and Mrs Everest, his old nurse, over the next few years, places the three adult characters in a distinct, if hardly ideal, pattern. In February 1890 the boy had received treatment for his toothache, supplemented by folk-remedy advice from Mrs Everest, who wrote:

I hope you have recovered from the effects of the dental opperation [sic]…
I hope you wear your coat this wet weather and change your Boots when
they are damp, that is what gives you toothache sitting in wet Boots.[7]

A year later, on or about 26 April 1891, Winston wrote to his mother from Harrow:

I have had an awful toothache ever since I got here

and the next day, it seems:

My face is swelled up double its natural size through toothache

4 Much of young Winston's medical education came in the form of folk-remedies proposed by his old nurse, Mrs Everest.

signing himself 'Your tooth tormented – but affectionate – son'. Mrs Everest was next to contribute, writing on 28 April:

I am so sorry about your toothache, poor darling. I went off early this morning 8 O'clock but the Dentist's Man said they were full up & could not possibly give you an appointment before Thursday at 5. Poor old Man – have you tried the heroine [? for Heroin – certainly opiates were freely available in dilute form in those days] I got you – get a bottle of Elliman's embrocation & rub your face when you go to bed & tie your sock up over your face, after rubbing for ¼ of an hour, try it I am sure it will do good.

On the Wednesday, 29 April, Lady Randolph came into the exchange, with her scolding advice:

I am *so* sorry to hear you have a toothache, & I hear from Everest that the dentist cannot see you until tomorrow. Perhaps he will pull it out. I don't want to lecture on the subject – but I am

> sure if you wld take a little more care of yr teeth you wd not suffer so
> much. Quite apart from the 'pigginess' of not brushing them!! However
> I do hope darling that you are better. I am quite settled here [Banstead
> Manor, near Newmarket] & like it very much

The problem dragged on, and on 11 June 1891 Mrs Everest had further folk-advice
to offer:

> How is your poor face ache. Did you go to the Dentist? Don't eat too
> many of those nasty pickles they are poisonous things. I hope you will
> enjoy your Chicken Pie & cake they won't hurt you.

A week later, on 17 June, she regretted that

> … Dr Pritchard said he would not undertake to extract a tooth he has
> not nerve enough now who is going to do it for you?

Meanwhile Winston had reported to his mother that

> I have got an appointment for 4.30 on Thursday afternoon with Dr
> Braine. Do come up & write and tell Welldon [his headmaster at
> Harrow] you will look after me & 'give me Tea.'
> I have had no more pain. Please do come I shall not like going alone at all.

Ultimately the tooth had to be extracted, in London under general anaesthesia.
The Braines (Charles Carter and his father Francis Woodhouse), who were called
in to deal with this situation, were leaders in dental anaesthesia in their time.

* * *

After two attempts at the Sandhurst entry examination, the youth was entrusted to
a crammer to prepare for a third. But in January 1893, holidaying in Bournemouth,
he was trying to evade his brother Jack and a cousin; they cornered him on a bridge
over a gully; he took a chance on being able to reach, and shin down, a young fir
tree growing alongside the bridge. He lost his grip, and fell about 9m [30 feet] on

to hard ground. He was unconscious for three days (which denotes a major head injury) and confined to bed for two or three months. (Two months in fact, but three in Churchill's account, given in *My early life*.)

When the doctors examined him,' according to Martin, 'they found a ruptured kidney'.[5] Presumably it was a period of haematuria (blood in the urine) with associated loin pain that drew their attention to the injury; at least the damage to his kidney must have been modest enough to validate a conservative approach. There was also an injury to his thigh, for the management of which the period of bed rest sufficed. Now 1895 was to be Röntgen's year, and Röntgen's x-rays were announced to the world at the very end of it;[6] so that it was not until Churchill broke his hip 70 years later that the 1893 femoral fracture was identified. It is hard to appreciate, in an era of sophisticated imaging, how obscure was the detail of the human body's internal condition prior to Röntgen's discovery.

* * *

With the help of the crammer over several months in mid-1893, Churchill succeeded in passing the Sandhurst exam at that third attempt: his father was highly critical because his son's mark did not qualify him for the infantry but only the cavalry. Entering the College in September 1893, he passed out (eighth in a class of 150, according to his account, not disputed by Broad, Moorehead or Best; but Gilbert and Pelling say 20th out of 130: either way, a creditable pass) at the end of the following year.

Further dental problems, and a crop of boils, had punctuated the early part of 1894. On 13 February Winston wrote to his mother:[7]

The boils are healing up and I do not think they will have to be lanced again. My tooth is still very troublesome but I think it will get better gradually.

It did not. On 19 February:

I had a fearful night on Saturday. The most awful toothache I have ever had. Not a wink of sleep – though I took two Sulphonels [sic].[8] Now however the nerve is dead & will give no more pain I hope.

15

The same day he wrote to his father:

> I have had a very bad time of it for the last week, especially during the latter part with my tooth. But now the nerve has been killed and so I am alright and shall I hope have no more trouble.

On 14 February Mrs Everest had made her contribution:

> Poor old boy I am so sorry you are troubled with tooth ache do get some spirits of camphor & rub some on your gums & also on your cheek frequently nothing so good for it… I hope the Boils are dying away.

This advice she supplemented a week later:

> I hope you have quite recovered from the Boils & that you are feeling stronger & better in health altogether. Take care of your health & don't tamper yourself with physic take plenty of open air exercise & you will not require Medicine. It will ruin your constitution also your interior such a mistake.

On the same day as her advice came a parental blast from Lord Randolph:

> I am glad that your tooth has at last been summarily dealt with. I strongly advise you to go to my old friend Pritchard 9 Albemarle St. You don't want to be having your teeth pulled out or having nerves killed & he will not do the one & if he does the other he will do it painlessly but as he likes me very much he will probably do anything for you & I will make an appointment with him for the first Saturday after the next on which you can get leave.

Of course we already know, from the dental crisis three years earlier, how Mrs Everest regarded Dr Pritchard.

* * *

Lord Randolph continued to be scathing of his son's endeavours, even of his medical problems. Thus, on 28 May 1894:

I am very glad to hear you have got out of hospital. Sick headaches sound very much like biliousness of which Roose would have cured you in 24 hours.

What Lord Randolph did not know was that his own state of health was the subject on which Roose had already written, on 4 May, to share his concerns with Thomas Buzzard, a leading neurologist:

Dear Dr Buzzard

I have seen Lord R.C. and in accordance with your letter I again asked for a consultation with you about his case, however he will not sanction another consultn. at present. Further I have this week written to my patient and stated that I considered he ought to give up public life at least for a while as I considered his nerve symptoms required rest, in that letter I also suggested a consultation. Do you not think we ought to write and jointly sign a letter to Lord R.C. urging that he should be guided by our advice and take a prolonged rest?

And what neither of the Churchills knew was that Lord Randolph was considered by his doctors to be in the grip of GPI, the letters denoting 'general paralysis of the insane', one of the manifestations of tertiary [late] syphilis – though perhaps, according to Simon Schama, his problem may have been 'some sort of wasting neural disease'[9] – whichever it was, he became aggressively irrational in the early stages. It was, moreover, a disease which would kill him a year later at the age of only 45.

Winston himself maintained a belief in the doctors' diagnosis. Montague Browne, his last Private Secretary, recalls that

Quite early in my service WSC said to me: 'You know my father died of locomotor ataxia, the child of syphilis.' The significance of this remark lies, of course, not in whether WSC was right or wrong, but in the fact that this was what he believed.[10]

Assuming syphilis, the spirochaetes must have entered him at a stage that could spare his wife and sons; Lady Randolph was to have two more husbands after

Lord Randolph's death – both of them about Winston's age – while Jack, five years younger than Winston and like him a premature baby, had a worthwhile career and died at the age of 67, five years before his daughter Clarissa became Anthony Eden's second wife.

> ### Table 2
>
> ## THE SECOND DECADE 1884-94
>
> Pneumonia
>
> Throat and liver complaints
>
> Concussion (fall from bicycle)
>
> Dental caries
>
> Boils
>
> Head injury, ruptured kidney, fractured femur (fall from tree)

NOTES

1 Harrow added a verse to the school song in 1940 in tribute to its famous son:

Nor less we praise in darker days
   The leader of our nation
And CHURCHILL's name shall win acclaim
   From each new generation.
While in this fight to guard the right
   Our country you defend, Sir,
Here grim and gay we mean to stay
   And stick it to the end, Sir.

Churchill substituted the word 'sterner' for 'darker' in the first line; and in 1941 Harrow altered four lines to reflect the war situation:

[For] you have [the] power in danger's hour
   Our freedom to defend, Sir:
Though long the fight, we know the right
   Will triumph in the end, Sir.

2 Gilbert [2004] p.11.

3 French, H (ed); *An index of differential diagnosis of main symptoms*. 1912 [3rd edn 1922] ; Bristol, John Wright. p.642.

4   Capper, KR (ed); *The extra Pharmacopoeia (Martindale)*. 1952; London: Pharmaceutical Press. p. 741.

5   Martin, H: *Battle: the life story of Winston S. Churchill*. 1941; London: Gollancz. p.23.

6   Röntgen's printed paper is dated 'Ende 1895', and was delivered to the Würzburg Physico-Medical Society on 28 December 1895 for publication in the society's Proceedings. Because of the holiday period the paper was available in printed form before Röntgen had presented his findings to his own university colleagues. One advance copy he sent to his former co-worker Franz Exner, now professor of physics in Vienna; and Exner showed the material to a gathering in his home. One of his guests was Ernst Lecher, a professor from Prague, who prevailed on Exner to lend him Röntgen's photographic plates overnight. But Lecher's father was the publisher of the *Vienna Press*, and Lecher was more loyal to his father than to the niceties of confidence. Lecher senior made sure that his paper enjoyed its scoop, on 5 January 1896 – to Röntgen's extreme embarrassment. Seventy years later Churchill's confidence would be similarly transgressed – by his physician.

7   The correspondence which follows, about Winston's general and dental health in the period 1891-4, is collected in Vol. 1a of the Companion Volume. Individual letters are on microfilm in the Churchill Archives Centre, Cambridge.

8   Sulphonal, not sulphonel. Indeed Martindale's account of sulphonal makes it plain that the drug was not indicated for young Winston's dental pain. It was a hypnotic capable of producing prolonged sleep 'in psychiatric cases and in nervous insomnia' but had 'no analgesic properties' and was thus 'of no value in insomnia due to pain'.

9   Schama, S: *A History of Britain*. 2002; London: BBC Worldwide. III: 403. On the other hand Geoffrey Best quotes Mather's suggestion of a brain tumour [Best, G: *Churchill – a study in greatness*. 2001; London: Penguin. Mather, JH: *Maladies et mort*; in *Finest Hour (Journal of the International Churchill Societies)* (1996): 93:23] The jury will be out for a long time on the subject of Lord Randolph; what can be said is that he treated his son with a blend of neglect and derision.

10   Montague Browne, A: *Long sunset*. 1995; London: Cassell. p.122.

III

A
PLEASING
EMANCIPATION

The life at Sandhurst is
a pleasing emancipation.

- WSC: essay in the *Pall Mall Magazine* (1896)

A part from an occasion when a ¾ mile run with rifle and pack proved too much for him (the doctor said there was nothing wrong 'except that my heart does not seem very strong', he reported) Sandhurst left young Winston unscathed; and in February 1895 he was commissioned into the 4th Hussars. Within a month, however, he had injured his knee – 'a resounding blow', he told his brother Jack – trying a horse on the steeplechase course.

Later that year Churchill and his friend Barnes managed to get themselves to Cuba, where the Spanish were confronting a rebellion; they travelled by way of New York and were treated with lavish respect wherever they went. Churchill had secured a commission from the *Daily Graphic* (for which his father had written) to send back reports 'from the Front', where he spent his twenty-first birthday and heard what would become a familiar sound, as 'bullets whistled over our heads'. In this, his first experience of warfare, he bore a charmed life; and he and his companion brought back a Spanish decoration apiece.[1]

His regiment went to India the following year. Until the early 1890s such voyages were made in Government troopships, but these had become old and decrepit, so that in 1894 the P & O liner *Britannia* and two consorts were chartered as replacements; 'Everyone,' wrote Frank C Bowen four decades later, 'was surprised at the result. Officers and troops were infinitely more comfortable in the passenger quarters of the passenger liners, and the cost to the Government was far less.'

Before leaving, Churchill consulted Dr Felix Semon, a leading laryngologist [the physician precursor of the ENT surgeon] about his speech defect, which made his Ss into SHs. Semon's report caught him up in India and he reported to his mother that 'practice and perseverance are alone necessary and… no organic defect exists'. (In later years, the defect proved its worth, when Churchill's after-dinner speeches came over with no extra slurring evident.)

Semon, later knighted, was a Prussian of Jewish family who became a very successful practitioner in London; he was a noted name-dropper, but he appears to have been impressed with the young Churchill. His autobiography lists a couple of pages of the rich and great after observing 'From a social point of view my practice became more and more interesting, and remained so until the end of my active career' – but he then goes on to record his recollection of Churchill's visit to him.

One day in 1890, after the end of my consulting hours, I said to my wife:
"I have just seen the most extraordinary young man I have ever met. He

is only sixteen years old, and is the eldest son of the late Lord Randolph Churchill. Without being handsome, his face is very intellectual. After informing me that he had just left Harrow, he added: 'I intend to go to Sandhurst, and afterwards to join a Regiment of Hussars in India. Of course it is not my intention to become a mere professional soldier. I only wish to gain some experience. Some day I shall be a statesman as my father was before me.'"[2]

The chronology is jumbled, the narrative doubtless 'improved'; but it suggests that Semon found his young visitor worth remembering.

* * *

Churchill soon had a more important disability to contend with. Interestingly he did not mention the original event in his letters home to his mother; but the autobiography *My Early Life* describes how, on arrival in Bombay, when he was approaching the dockside in a small skiff with two colleagues,

We came alongside of a great stone wall with dripping steps and iron rings for handholds. The boat rose and fell 4 or 5 feet with the surges. I put out my hand and grasped at a ring; but before I could get my feet on the steps the boat swung away, giving my right shoulder a sharp and peculiar wrench. I scrambled up all right, made a few remarks... hugged my shoulder and soon thought no more about it... Since then my shoulder has dislocated on the most unexpected pretexts.[3]

A letter home to his mother, dated 5 January 1898, describes one such event:

You must excuse my handwriting as I have dislocated my shoulder at polo – and am all strapped up. So painful it was – and I fear may ultimately end my polo career for it may slip out again

Reflecting three decades later on the condition of his shoulder, Churchill went on to describe how

Once it very nearly went out through a too expansive gesture in the House of Commons, and I thought how astonished the members would have been to see the speaker to whom they were listening, suddenly for no reason throw himself upon the floor in an instinctive effort to take the strain and leverage off the displaced arm-bone.[3]

A shoulder dislocation is one of the classic injuries: it was dealt with by Hippocrates in his writings, and the Hippocratic method of reduction is still practised. It requires that 'the operator, seizing with his hand the affected arm, is to pull it, while with his heel in the armpit he pushes in the contrary direction'.

5 Hippocrates' method of reducing a dislocation of the shoulder, with the aid of a foot planted in the armpit, is still employed after more than two millennia. This illustration is from a 1607 work by de Croce.

But Hippocrates went further; he wrote also on recurrent dislocation of the shoulder, for which he recommended the application of the cautery to the front of the shoulder, for long enough to burn through the tissues into which the head of the humerus displaced; then

When the sores have become clean and are going on to cicatrisation, then by all means the arm is bound to the side night and day; and even when the ulcers are completely healed the arm must still be bound to the side for a long time; for thus… the wide space into which the humerus used to escape will be contracted.[4]

6a As early as 1890 Broca and Hartmann described and illustrated the structural defects that predispose to recurrence of shoulder dislocations: this horizontal section through a shoulder (with the front of the joint to the bottom of the diagram) shows the capsule of the joint [C] stripped off the shoulder blade at [P] to create a loose 'pocket'; and an associated defect in the head of the humerus [T] which has allowed it to slip forward into this pocket from its normal position in the shallow 'cup' of the glenoid [G].

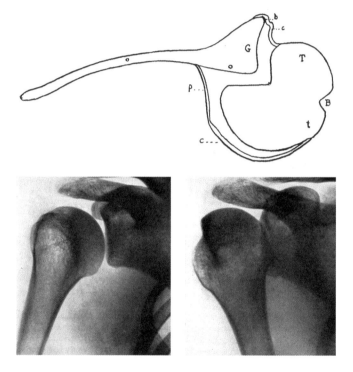

6b In the x-ray on the left, the head of the humerus appears normally rounded, but when the arm is rotated to bring the defect into profile, it becomes very plain to see.

It is interesting to note that the Hippocratic principles remain valid (even if orthopaedics today employs other and gentler methods than the cautery for limiting external rotation laxity), and it would be fair to say that neglect of this principle – as in the Nicola procedure of 1929, which sought to insert a strip of ligament as a tether into the joint – carries its own reward.[5]

We may wonder, of course, why Churchill did not seek surgical treatment of his recurrent dislocation even at the time [1930] he wrote his autobiography, given the embarrassments he then described. The operations described by Blundell Bankart in 1923, and by Vittorio Putti (also 1923) and Harry Platt (1925, the same procedure independently arrived at) were well enough established:[6] but perhaps after three decades Churchill had become sufficiently reconciled to the disorder.

7 In London, Blundell Bankart [left] described his operation for repair of a recurrent shoulder dislocation in 1923, a time when Churchill was out of Parliament and could have been 'available', while Harry Platt [right] of Manchester described an alternative method of repair two years later

* * *

In the spring of 1897 came one of a number of military 'near misses': Churchill was in the butts of a rifle range, supervising the target-markers. A round struck the metal frame of the target, showering him with splinters. As he described it, in a letter to his mother, dated 6 April 1897:

> **In Cuba it was my fortune to be under fire, without being wounded. At Bangalore I have been wounded without being under fire... One [splinter] entered my left hand near the thumb and penetrated an inch and a half... It is to the mercy of God... that I was not hit in the eye... Followed an abominable twenty minutes – probing etc – before the splinter was extracted & since then I have had a bad time**

every morning when the wound has to be syringed. Knowing, as you do, my keen aversion to physical pain or even discomfort I am sure you will sympathise with me… However I am healing beautifully and yesterday I managed to play polo with the reins fastened to my wrist, so that you can see I am not really very bad.

In the field, on the other hand, he bore a charmed life: he took part in the Malakand Field Force's operations on the North-West Frontier, north of Peshawar (and wrote a book about them); he served with the Tirah expedition. Then, hungry for adventure and fame, he secured a posting to Kitchener's operation against the Khalifa's army in the Sudan.[7] Kitchener did not want him, especially as he had a contract to write for the *Morning Post*; but he got himself posted to the 21st Lancers, and took part with them in the cavalry charge at Omdurman on 2 September 1898. 'On account of my shoulder,' he recorded,

I had always decided that if I were involved in hand-to-hand fighting I must use a pistol and not a sword. I had purchased in London a Mauser automatic pistol, then the newest and latest design.

And he reflected that

Perhaps if… I had been able to use a sword… my story might not have got so far as the telling…. Life is a whole, and luck is a whole, and no part of them can be separated from the rest.[8]

In Cairo afterwards, he provided some of his skin for a graft, to cover a wound above the right wrist suffered by his colleague Richard Molyneux: it is curious that (although Churchill describes the removal of the skin from the inner aspect of his forearm) the normally meticulous Gilbert has it coming from Churchill's chest. I suspect he is mixing this up with the penknife incident at school.[9]

In 1899 he returned briefly to India, long enough to play in the winning team in the Inter-Regimental polo tournament at Meerut (his arm strapped to his side on account of a recent recurrence of his shoulder dislocation – but he did score three of the goals that enabled his side to win the final 4-3) before resigning his commission in order to enter politics.[10] He left behind an unpaid bill for 13 rupees at the Bangalore Club: the ancient ledger recording this 'irrecoverable debt' is proudly displayed in the club.

8 To minimise the risk of a recurrence of his shoulder dislocation, Churchill employed a splint which would keep his arm to his side when he played polo [which he did until the age of 50; this photograph was taken in 1921]   In the cavalry charge at Omdurman he had taken the precaution of using a pistol in preference to a sword.

On his way back to England, he stopped in Egypt long enough to acquire necessary detail for his account of the recent campaign, which came out as *The River War*, and contains perceptive observations on militant Islam that read, a century later, like the better sort of contemporary journalism.

Back home he contested a by-election for the Oldham seat in Lancashire, but was unsuccessful; and when war broke out in South Africa he hastened to get himself out there as a war correspondent for the *Morning Post*. He travelled out in *Dunottar Castle*, along with the incoming commander-in-chief, General Sir Redvers Buller VC, both men fretting that the war might be over before they arrived. They need not have worried.

Churchill reached Capetown on 31 October, and by 15 November he was on his third trip by armoured train up towards the Boer force that was besieging Ladysmith. The Boers ambushed and partially derailed the train and Churchill – naturally – was soon running the show. He got the engine, and a number of wounded, safely away back towards the British forces, then set out to rejoin the rest of the party.[11] He did not make it; and he found himself, along with the other members of the train party, imprisoned in Pretoria.[12]

9 After his escape from a Boer prisoner of war camp, Churchill was given a commission in The South African Light Horse. He returned on 24 December 1899 to the scene of the ambush of the armoured train.

Four weeks later he escaped; he was befriended by an English mine manager, who hid him underground until he could make his way east to Lourenco Marques hidden among bales of wool on a freight train. Three days underground in the mine provided his worst experience: Gilbert records that a local doctor, James Gillespie, 'let into the secret,... advised that he be brought up to the surface, as he had become "very nervy"'[13] - which probably means claustrophobia and a panic attack. Certainly confinement underground, in darkness and with only the resident white rats for company, is an experience well calculated to produce such an attack; but by the time Churchill wrote about his escape later it had become more of an adventure, and he identified 'an English doctor twenty miles away' only as the source of a roast chicken with which he was provided during his time underground. 'Luckily for me,' he wrote, 'I have no horror of rats as such, and… I was not particularly uneasy. All the same, the three days I passed in the mine were not among the most pleasant which my memory re-illumines'.[14]

He was in Durban for Christmas, and began the New Year with a commission in the South African Light Horse. He was with the relief column into Ladysmith, and his report to the *Morning Post* made him a celebrity back home. When he returned to England in July 1900 he was promptly adopted as the Tory candidate for Oldham – and this time he was triumphantly if narrowly elected.

But it was not long before he fell out with the Conservative party on the issue of Free Trade. By 1904 the Liberals of NW Manchester had secured his agreement to stand as their Free Trade candidate; and then on 22 April came a curious episode. He had been speaking in a debate on a Trade Union Bill. Thirty years later he described the event, in a newspaper essay dated 12 May 1934 (which he entitled 'When I "dried up"')

I had spoken for three quarters of an hour in a good House with a considerable measure of success. I had reached my last sentence for which my note was: 'And it rests with those who…' Suddenly my memory failed! I could not for the life of me recall who it was that this important matter rested with.

Because this was planned to be his final sentence he could not skip to the next; and after two repetitions of the cue he was still without inspiration. After his discomfiture, as he reported, had been 'endured by the House with the greatest patience and kindness, I had to sit down, faltering out some lame apology'.

His fellow-members noted that, after he had began a sentence, he 'hesitated, seeming to search for words… stopped speaking, appeared confused, fumbled through his notes, and sat down… he covered his face with his hands and muttered 'I thank Hon Members for having listened to me.'[15]

Colleagues recalled with dismay his father's decline into incoherence; Jack Seely, his kindred spirit in the House, sent him a letter from a Dr G H R Dabbs (who combined the skills of a medical practitioner with those of a novelist, playwright and horse breeder, and who – according to Seely's covering letter – 'used to be considered a great authority on the brain'):

> **Very sorry (but not surprised for I expect he has overdone his nervous system) to read of Mr W Churchill's attack of defective cerebration: it comes to the readiest at times… It is a strange experience to those who *have* experienced it. Luckily it hardly ever recurs. My view of it is that it is sudden brain anaemia: a sort of syncope of the memory cells.[16]**

The encouraging item in Dabbs' analysis is his assertion that recurrence is unlikely. The experience did, however, prompt Churchill to provide himself with full notes throughout his political career.

Table 3

THE THIRD DECADE 1894-1904
Knee injury (steeplechasing)
Speech defect assessed (Semon)
Dislocation right shoulder (later recurrent)
Laceration thumb (metal fragment)
Skin graft donor
Claustrophobia and panic attack
Fugue

NOTES

1 Gilbert describes this as 'a Spanish military decoration, the Red Cross.' I would interpret this as an award of the 1st class of the Military Order of Merit, which has two divisions (war services, and military service in general), of which the former has a red-enamelled cross and a red ribbon with a central white stripe – in the latter division, the colours are reversed. Unlike most orders, this has the most junior of its four grades designated the '1st class'. Churchill's portrait by Sir John Lavery has such a ribbon.

It may be noted that he brought back two other cultural refinements: the siesta, which enabled him to work much longer hours than seemed otherwise possible, and a lifetime devotion to Havana cigars, which became a part of his dramatic persona, more perhaps than providing a source of nicotine.

2 Semon, H & McIntyre TA (eds) *The autobiography of Sir Felix Semon KCVO, MD, FRCP*. 1926; London: Jarrold. p.191.

3 Churchill [1944]; p.110-111.

4 Hippocrates (trans. Adams, F 1849) *The genuine works*. London: Sydenham Society.

5 The Nicola procedure, according to a series quoted by Nicholson, [*Journal of Bone & Joint Surgery* (1950): 32B: 511] resulted in 21 failures from 59 cases (35%), as compared with 5.5% for the Bankart procedure and 5.4% for the Putti-Platt. It seems to have produced a stiff but stable shoulder until the contrived 'ligament' chafed through, after which movement and instability alike were regained.

6 Bankart identified a tearing-away of the front lip of the shoulder socket, and set out to re-attach this. Putti and Platt, on the other hand, 'double-breasted' the lax tissues across the front of the joint, producing in effect the strong scar of Hippocrates' cautery.

7   As Guedalla described it, 'Sir Herbert Kitchener, Sirdar of the Egyptian Army, was moving south with six brigades in the Sudan to end the Mahdist nightmare and avenge Gordon.' [*Mr Churchill*, (1941): London: Hodder & Stoughton, p. 65] The Mahdi, leader of a fanatical uprising, had besieged General 'Chinese' Gordon in Khartoum in 1885, taking the city and killing Gordon two days before the arrival of a relief column. He had submitted Gordon's corpse to indignities that Britain found hard to tolerate; regrettably Kitchener desecrated the Mahdi's tomb with equal savagery after his victory at Omdurman (and that, the young Churchill found hard to tolerate; so that *The River war* carried its share of criticism). At the outbreak of the First War in 1914, Churchill was First Lord of the Admiralty, Kitchener his army counterpart as War Minister: history is full of such ironies.

8   Churchill [1944]: p.111.

9   Gilbert, M [2004]: 1991; p.112 (see also p.8). Moran confirms the site from which the graft was taken, describing how Churchill showed him the scar at the time of Molyneux's death in 1954.

10   He did not, however, retire from polo for many years. As Guedalla commented, writing of Churchill's term as War Minister in 1919,
His faithful secretary concealed his master's healthy taste for polo among the sober round of his official appointments under the discreet alias… of 'Collective Equitation.' Few ministers play polo at forty-four. But Mr Churchill retained his vigour.

11   Churchill did not forget the courage shown by the crew of the engine and, having written as an individual to the editor of *The Spectator* without effect at the time, he had the satisfaction of getting the Albert Medal awarded to the driver (1st class, equivalent to the George Cross) and fireman (2nd class) in 1910, when his commendation had his ministerial status to support it.

12 His captor was Louis Botha, who would become the first post-war prime minister of the Transvaal and, in 1910, the first premier of the newly-formed Union of South Africa. 'He and I have been out in all weathers,' Botha assured Lady Randolph when they met in 1906; the two men became firm friends and worked well together prior to and during the First War.

13 Gilbert [2004] p. 135. When Churchill escaped, the Boers offered a reward of £25 for his capture, alive or dead, describing him as an Englishman of 'average build, walks with a slight stoop, pale appearance, red brown hair, small and hardly noticeable moustache, talks through his nose and cannot pronounce the letter S properly'.

14 Churchill, *My Early Life*. pp.300-301.

15 Gilbert [2004] p.185.

16 The correspondence is printed in Companion volume 2/1 of the Randolph Churchill / Martin Gilbert biography, p.339.

IV

THE FLEET WAS READY

There is one thing at any rate
they cannot take from you.
The Fleet was ready.

- Kitchener to WSC: May 1915

A year after the embarrassing scene in the House Churchill suffered a further collapse, took himself off to his aunt's home in Dorset, and there found a masseuse who, as he told his mother, had 'almost miraculous virtues & I am very comfortable & peaceful.' We can judge the masseuse by the fact that she found his tongue 'restrained by a ligament *which nobody else has*' [always a revealing term, this one]. He consulted Sir Felix Semon again, who refused to cut his 'tongue-tie'.

But 1908 was a better year. Not only did he become a member of Asquith's Cabinet, as President of the Board of Trade, but on 12 September he married Clementine Hozier, ten years his junior. The final sentence of *My early life* reads, 'Events were... to absorb my thoughts and energies... until September 1908, when I married and lived happily ever afterwards.' It was indeed, and was to remain a happy match and durable, between two people of strong character and will. And although he was defeated in the by-election for Manchester North West that was (under the rules of the time) obligatory on joining the Cabinet, he was elected as Liberal member for Dundee.

10 Churchill married Clementine Hozier in 1908. This was their engagement photograph. In his autobiography he noted that he 'married and lived happily ever afterwards'.

In 1909, however, he fell foul of the suffragettes and their supporters. As he and Clementine got off the train in Bristol where he had a speaking engagement, a certain Theresa Garnett attacked him with a dog whip. To protect his face he grabbed her wrists, whereupon she tried to push him off the platform in the path of the now moving train. Clementine was able to grab his coat and pull him back from the edge. The following year a suffragette supporter, one Hugh Franklin, attacked Churchill – also with a whip – on a train from Bradford to London. It would seem that the more militant suffragettes were the lineal ancestors of today's animal liberationists, prepared to kill and destroy in pursuit of what they regard as a just cause.

More to Churchill's liking he was, that same year of 1910, appointed Home Secretary. It was not an easy post, with rioting in the Welsh valleys and, in January 1911, 'the battle of Sidney Street' when three anarchist burglars killed three of the six policemen who were trying to arrest them. They then took refuge in an East End house where they killed a fourth policeman. Lacking accurate information, Churchill went to see for himself what was happening – and this, naturally enough, gave his critics scope for accusing him of interfering. In fact the nearest he came to interfering was when the terrorists set fire to the house, and the fire brigade (in accord with their standing orders) prepared to fight the blaze. Since the terrorists were shooting at everything in sight, Churchill endorsed the Police instruction to the firemen, to stand well back and let the fire take its course.[1]

* * *

In July 1911 Churchill wrote to his wife, describing how he had dined with his cousin's wife Alice Guest the previous night, and reported that she

> **...interested me a great deal by her talk about her doctor in Germany, who completely cured her depression. I think this man might be useful to me – if my black dog returns. He seems to be quite away from me now – it is such a relief. All the colours come back into the picture.[2]**

The whole question of depression, the black dog and so on has shown a tendency to get out of hand, and I think it merits examination.

We could start with the proposition that Churchill was of what has been called 'mercurial temperament', but will that serve? – The [Oxford English Reference] Dictionary defines 'mercurial' as: '(of a person) sprightly, ready-witted, volatile', and later it expands 'volatile' with three shades of meaning: '2. changeable, fickle. 3. lively, light-hearted. 4. apt to break out into violence'. These several definitions thus conjure up quite varied, even contrasting, shades of meaning, and fail to depict Churchill with any precision.

Perhaps Ian Hay's sketch of the personality of Eric Bethune in *The willing Horse* has more to offer:

> **Eric's old Scottish nurse was accustomed to say of him that he was "aye up in the cloods or doon in the midden."[3]**

And mood swings are a common enough feature of the driven man. Of John Hunter, 'the founder of scientific surgery', his biographer Stephen Paget wrote that he was

> **emotional and impetuous – quickly moved to tears of sympathy, quickly ablaze with anger and fierce word.[4]**

Harold Edwards, a medical brigadier who met Churchill in 1945, saw something similar in him; describing Churchill's eyes, he diaried that

> **… they can be hard as he looks at you – or as tender as a woman's – they can weep easily. I believe now the story of how he cried – how he wept – as described by M. Herriot, when he realised all was lost in France. He is emotional – not "Irishly" so. I think the right description is that he allows himself to react fully and without restraint and without troubling himself what impression he makes on the onlooker. He is no actor, no poseur.[5]**

The challenge is to determine whether the mood swings of the 'normal' person are part of a continuous spectrum which leads from torpor at one extreme to mania at the other. If there is a spectrum, the next requirement is to determine at what point on it personality becomes abnormal; and if this can be done, it is then necessary to place Churchill on the spectrum, and decide whether he belongs on the normal or the abnormal side of this threshold.

Recent campaigns to make mental illness 'respectable' in New Zealand – a worthy aim, to be sure – have included, in their television advertising, a photograph of Churchill as a celebrated sufferer from depression *as a mental illness*. But such advertising overlooks the fact that, even in Churchill's later years, depression seems to have been viewed as a symptom rather than a diagnosis. I have quoted previously from the BMA series of essays entitled *Refresher course for general practitioners* as providing a convenient snapshot of medical opinion from the 1950s. There an essay on *The anxiety-state* by Dr E.A. Bennet MD ScD DPM, physician to the Bethlem Royal and Maudsley Hospital, includes the comment that

> **Depression is more frequent than any other symptom in the anxiety-state, but so it is also in melancholia, schizophrenia, and in some organic diseases such as pre-senile dementia and arteriosclerosis. Patients usually deny that they are depressed and it is better to enquire whether they have less energy than they had before. Depression is generally accompanied by a diminution of energy, and a lack of resilience and enterprise. New work and new problems are distasteful. Many experience fluctuations of energy with concurrent depression and this appears to be part of their constitutional makeup. In others the fluctuation is less prominent or absent and the depression may be associated with disturbing circumstances. Depression is therefore an important symptom and when it is severe and when the frame of mind contrasts sharply with what the patient describes as his normal outlook, it is essential to take a dated history, noticing, in particular, previous periods when similar symptoms were present.[6]**

This places depression firmly in the category of a symptom, even several decades after the period when Churchill himself used the term 'the black dog'.

I think his physician, Charles McMoran Wilson, Lord Moran, must be given credit (if that is the word) for bringing this term to public view as *evidence of depression as a disease*.[7] In the work which brought him celebrity and opprobrium in about equal doses, he recorded his version of the remarks of his famous patient:

> **"When I was young," the P.M. ruminated, "a black depression settled on me for two or three years. It helped me to talk to Clemmie about it.**

> **I still don't like standing near the edge of a platform when an express train is passing through. I don't like to stand by the side of a ship and look down into the water. A second's action would end everything. And yet I don't want to go out of the world at all in such moments.**[8]

Read carefully, this comment tells of prudent self-protection more than suicidal thoughts – after the episode of the suffragette, who would wish to flirt with trains? Yet it was on such bases that Moran built his edifice of recurrent depression as a mental illness.

Geoffrey Best, one of Churchill's highly-regarded biographers, accepts Moran's diagnosis, but with a grain of salt. He writes:

> **Much has been written about this [depression, the 'black dog'] since it became public knowledge in the book his personal physician Lord Moran published very soon after he died, but its importance has been exaggerated. It never stopped him doing whatever he wanted to do.**[9]

That final sentence sums it up: depression-as-a-disease inflicts a sense of hopeless lethargy on its sufferers – and Churchill's black dog was not such a disorder.

Churchill's official biographer, Martin Gilbert, also pondered the matter of depression. It worried him that 'as a result of the publication of his doctor's diary in 1965, the picture of Churchill as frequently and debilitatingly depressed had, by the time I began my work, taken hold in the general literature'. He consulted, therefore, with colleagues who had been close enough to Churchill to be reliable witnesses. From Jock (Sir John) Colville he received a letter in April 1969:

> **I suppose that this hypothetical state of depression into which Lord Moran alleges Sir Winston used to fall will become accepted dogma. I therefore, some time ago, took the trouble to ask Lady Churchill about the theory. She was quite positive that although her husband was occasionally depressed – as indeed most normal people are – he was not abnormally subject to long fits of depression.**
>
> **The expression 'to have a black dog on one's back' was one that my nanny used to use very frequently. I suppose that Mrs Everest must have**

used it too. It was a very common expression among nannies. I think that Sir Winston must have said on various occasions to Lord Moran: 'I have got a black dog on my back today.' Lord Moran, not moving very frequently in nanny circles, evidently thought that this was some new and remarkable expression which Sir Winston applied to himself.

If I am right – and Lady Churchill thinks I am – this does show what dangerous errors historians can make, by being ignorant of the jargon of an age preceding their own.[10]

Since Colville served two significant terms as Churchill's Private Secretary, his opinion of Churchill's temperament, and also of Lady Churchill's objectivity, can be trusted. Even his supposition about Moran's line of thinking is confirmed by Moran himself:

He called his fits of depression the "black dog." I said, "You inherited the 'black dog' business from your forebears. You have fought against it all your life. That is why you dislike visiting hospitals. You always avoid anything that is depressing."[8]

What is more, the term 'black dog' goes back long before its appearance in nanny-speak; it was applied by Doctor Johnson, in a letter to Mrs Thrale, to his own periods of melancholy. That letter was written on 28 June 1783, ten days after Johnson had suffered a small stroke and been rendered briefly speechless. It is interesting that the editor of *The Oxford Dictionary of Quotations* comments on this matter:

More recently associated with Winston Churchill, who used the phrase 'black dog' when alluding to his own periodic bouts of depression.[11]

Neither the editor concerned, nor of course Lord Moran, would seem to have been aware of the 19th century 'nanny-speak' link between Johnson in the 18th century and Churchill in the 20th. And both Johnson, writing in the aftermath of a stroke, and Churchill with his own setbacks, had good enough cause to be melancholic; they are more easily accommodated in the category of depression-as-a-phenomenon than of depression-as-a-disease.

On the strength of all this, I am prepared to place Churchill well into the normal part of that spectrum to which I referred at the outset. The recent move by 'mental health charity Rethink' – to commission a statue of Churchill in a straitjacket 'to highlight the stigma of the illness' – has angered members of the Churchill family. In piling falsehood upon myth the charity has merely succeeded in stigmatising itself.

But the extent to which the 'black dog' has run wild provides an indictment of the extent to which Lord Moran's speculations also ran wild. An essay by Anthony Storr, an Oxford psychiatrist, appears in two guises – in Storr's own book *Churchill's Black Dog, Kafka's Mice & other phenomena of the Human Mind* and (apparently verbatim) as one chapter in a book entitled *Churchill: four faces and the man*. In this essay Storr explains, interprets, dissects various elements in Churchill's career and personality, before admitting that

> **It is at this point that psychoanalytic insight reveals its inadequacy. For, although I believe that the evidence shows that the conclusions reached in this chapter are justified, we are still at a loss to understand Churchill's remarkable courage.**[12]

And if you cannot explain or understand Churchill's courage, you cannot claim to have understood Churchill at all.

* * *

We left Churchill back in July 1911, confiding to his wife a possible solution to his low moments. But before the end of that year he became First Lord of the Admiralty, a role in which he revelled, into which he threw himself with the blend of commitment and sheer *joie de vivre* that characterised his enthusiasms; and in which he was able to achieve a state of naval preparedness at the outbreak of the First War that drew grudging approval even from his critics. During his time as First Lord he spent eight months aboard the Admiralty yacht, *Enchantress*, visiting naval establishments and ships in order to familiarise himself with the service of which he was the political head.

11 To get to grips with his task as First Lord of the Admiralty Churchill spent no less than eight months aboard the Admiralty yacht *Enchantress* after taking up his post in 1911. The level of preparedness of the fleet in August 1914 was taken as evidence of his achievement.

Two of his initiatives stand out. On the eve of war, he finalised a project to buy, on behalf of the British government, a majority shareholding in the Anglo-Persian Oil Company, and so 'secured for the Royal Navy the fuel oil vital for its warships, and made a handsome profit for the Exchequer in addition';[13] and on 26 July 1914 he and his First Sea Lord, Prince Louis of Battenberg, halted the dispersal of the two battle squadrons which were concentrated in the Channel after taking part in the test mobilisation that had replaced the normal naval manoeuvres of that tense summer.[14]

Table 4

THE FOURTH DECADE 1904-14

Attacks by whip-wielding suffragette and supporter
Depression (as in the 'black dog')

NOTES

1   This is stated by Hugh Martin, who was there. [Martin, H: *Battle: the life story of Winston S Churchill*. 1941: London, Gollancz. p. 72.]

2   Gilbert [2004] p.260.

3   Hay, I [Maj-Gen John Hay Beith]; *The willing Horse – a novel*. 1924: London, Hodder & Stoughton. p.63.

4   Paget, S; *John Hunter*. 1897: London; Unwin.

5   Quoted in Gilbert [2004] p. 992.

6   Bennet, E A ; The anxiety-state. In *Refresher course for general practitioners; 3rd collection*. 1956: London; BMA. p.537-8. Bennet, writing in this series, may be read as representing mainstream psychiatric opinion of the time.

7   My reservations about depression-as-disease have been reinforced by the paper 'Depression: epidemic or pseudo-epidemic?' by Summerfield, of the Institute of Psychiatry at King's College, London [*J R Soc Med* 2006: 99: 161]. There the author observes that, 'For a start, the term 'depression' tends to be used without qualification, as if it was settled that we were always referring to a free-standing biologically-based disorder. Yet in everyday usage, as much by doctors as by the general public, 'depression' can mean something figurative or literal, can denote a normal or abnormal state, and if abnormal either an individual symptom or a full-blown disorder. And though depression-as-disease may have acquired the status of a natural science category, this was an achievement rather than a discovery.' Later in the paper, commenting on the World Health Organisation's description of it as 'an epidemic that within two decades will be second only to cardiovascular disease in terms of global disease burden' he points out that '"depression" has no exact equivalent in non-Western cultures' and contends that 'there is no such thing as depression, if by this we mean (as the WHO appear to mean) a unitary, universally valid, pathological entity requiring medical intervention.'

8   Moran, Charles Wilson, Lord; *Winston Churchill – the struggle for survival 1940-1965*. 1966; London: Heron Books [originally published 1965; London: Constable].

9   Best, G; *Churchill: a study in greatness*. 2001; London: Hambledon and London. p.143.

10   Gilbert, M; *In search of Churchill*. 1994; London: Harper Collins. p.209.

11   Partington, A (ed) *The Oxford Dictionary of Quotations*. Revised 4th edn. 1996. Oxford & New York. p. 368; 17.

12   Storr, A; *Churchill's Black Dog, Kafka's Mice & other phenomena of the human Mind*. 1965; New York, Ballantine Books edn 1990. See also: *Churchill: four faces and the man*. 1969; London: Allen Lane.

13   Gilbert [1994]: p.5.

14   There is a delicious irony in the fact that this test mobilisation had been chosen to replace the normal summer manoeuvres – in the interests of economy. Thrift, whether in the expenditure of materials or of men, flew out the window after 1914.

V

YOUR STAR WILL RISE AGAIN

I do not doubt that your
star will rise again.

- Dr Welldon (headmaster of Harrow) to WSC, 1922

War with Germany and the Central Powers began on 4 August 1914 and within a few weeks Belgium was invaded; it was soon evident that trench warfare in France and Flanders offered few dividends and heavy casualties.

Churchill was one who looked for other more productive approaches; one, which dated from February 1915, began with the title 'landships' (as befitted an initiative of a First Lord).[1] It was indeed begun in Churchill's bedroom, at a time when he was suffering from a bad attack of influenza; and of all the innovations of that war the tank contributed most to land warfare.

About the same time, with Russia needing all the help she could get, an operation that could open up a supply line by way of the Black Sea held out the prospect of taking Turkey out of the struggle while supporting the Russian effort. From this idea emerged the Gallipoli campaign; but the execution of it lacked the inspiration of the idea itself.[2] First came a naval attempt to force the Dardanelles (which was called off, by the timid deputy of an ailing admiral, at the moment when the final Turkish minefield had been breached – at some cost, admittedly, in ageing battleships). Then, after Turkey had been given ample warning, came a land assault on the Gallipoli peninsula which, poorly planned and commanded, struggled throughout 1915 before the only well-conducted part of the campaign, an evacuation carried out with flair.[3]

There had to be a scapegoat, and Churchill was targeted; he was driven from office and spent six months from November 1915 in France, where (after a chilly welcome from a Grenadier Guards battalion to which he was attached for a start)[4] he commanded the 6th Royal Scots Fusiliers for much of the period. He flirted with death, as everyone did who served in the front line; but his flirtations were especially colourful.

In his first month in the trenches he was ordered to present himself at a certain point to be picked up by car and taken to meet the Corps commander; he waited in vain, to be informed later that the car had been 'driven off' by shells, but that it did not matter because the general had only wanted a chat 'and another day would do equally well'. He trudged back, irate, into the front line to find that his dugout had been struck by a shell not long after he left for his rendezvous. 'When I saw the ruin', he wrote, 'I was not so angry with the general after all.'

On another occasion when his dugout was damaged by a shell, one fragment struck the electric lantern that Churchill had been examining, almost splitting the battery holder in two and lodging within a couple of inches of his wrist. 'If it had been any nearer', wrote his 18-year old adjutant Jock MacDavid, who was hit on the finger by another fragment, 'it would certainly have taken off his wrist.'[5]

In May 1916 the remnants of his battalion were amalgamated into another division; he did not seek another command, but returned to his parliamentary duties. He fretted while Asquith was driven into retirement, hoped for office in the government of his friend Lloyd George; but until the following year the malign influence of his enemies kept him in the wilderness. Not until July 1917 was he given a ministerial post, as Minister of Munitions.

Eighteen months later he returned to the Cabinet to take over the War Office, with the task first of all of managing the demobilisation of Britain's wartime armies. His portfolio included the Air Ministry, and the temptation to resume flying himself (he had been learning before the war) soon overcame him: on 18 July 1919, not surprisingly, he managed to make a crash landing. His seat belt held him until the wrecked craft slowed down; his instructor turned off the fuel before impact. He was bruised, the instructor briefly knocked out. He learned his lesson (and although, one war later, his uniform as an honorary Air Commodore displayed pilot's wings from mid-1943 onwards, he never obtained a pilot's licence.)

* * *

At the beginning of 1921 Churchill was appointed Colonial Secretary. The portfolio brought with it two explosive issues: Ireland and the Middle East. The latter question was addressed at a conference in Cairo in March 1921. Churchill had with him a number of experts: T E Lawrence – Lawrence of Arabia – as his adviser on Arabian Affairs; Sir Percy Cox, the High Commissioner in Iraq; and Gertrude Bell, a noted orientalist (who, as Lawrence wrote to her father after her death in 1926, had 'given her life to Iraq… I don't think I ever met anyone more entirely civilised, in the sense of her width of intelligent sympathy'.)

On a 'lay day' during the meeting Churchill and Clementine, with Lawrence and Gertrude Bell, took a camel ride to view the Sphinx. Churchill's camel threw him, grazing his hand badly; but he remounted and went on to make several sketches at Saqqara (site of the original 'step' pyramid) before riding home on his now more agreeable camel.

The conference achieved enough to prompt even that fastidious critic, Lawrence, to observe [in a footnote in the *Seven Pillars of Wisdom*] that

12 During the 1921 Cairo conference Churchill, with Clementine, Gertrude Bell and T E Lawrence, visited the Sphinx and Pyramids. Churchill's camel threw him, injuring his hand, but this did not stop him from sketching in the area of the Saqqara step pyramid.

In a few weeks, at his conference in Cairo, he made straight all the tangle, finding solutions fulfilling (I think) our promise in letter and spirit (where humanly possible) without sacrificing any interest of our Empire or any interest of the peoples involved. So we were quit of the wartime Eastern adventure, with clean hands, but three years too late to earn the gratitude which peoples, if not states, can pay.[6]

The problems of Ireland became the next issue for Churchill to address. Here too he achieved much, and earned the respect of the men with whom he had to negotiate. The Sinn Fein leaders, Arthur Griffith and

Michael Collins, signed a treaty in the small hours of 6 December 1921; and over the objections of de Valera (the President of the Irish Parliament and a fervent Republican) a slender majority of his Cabinet voted to accept it, and proceed to the inauguration of the Irish Free State. The Commons in turn accepted the proposed treaty, despite a walk-out by a group of Tory diehards. Collins sent a message to Churchill: 'Tell Winston we could never have done anything without him.'

And then things went horribly wrong: in June 1922 Sir Henry Wilson, a former CIGS and a resolute Ulster Unionist, was shot dead in the street by a Republican gunman, while in Dublin de Valera incited disorder and the Republicans first seized the Four Courts building, then burned it when attacked by Collins's troops. In August Collins himself was assassinated.

It is an intriguing thought that, during Churchill's tenure of the post of Colonial Secretary, both Ireland and the Middle East came, albeit briefly, about as close to peace as they have done before or since.

* * *

The tensions between the parties were now such that Lloyd George's wartime coalition soon fell apart and, in October 1922, a general election became necessary when all but 88 of the Tories chose to withdraw their support. Churchill was unable to plead for a more prolonged loyalty to Lloyd George: he had developed right-sided abdominal pain three days before the Carlton Club meeting which took the decision to sink the coalition; and on the night of 18 October 1922 he underwent an operation for appendicitis, performed by Sir Crisp English. He was emerging from the anaesthetic as the meeting took place.

Appendicitis can certainly present at the most awkward times. Two decades earlier, when the condition was still widely known as 'perityphlitis' and its surgical management was in its infancy, the newly acceded King Edward VII was afflicted. He was seen by Frederick Treves, lately returned from service in the South African War; and it is reported that, when the king was told that he should undergo an operation, he burst out: 'But I must keep faith with my people: I am to go to the Abbey in two weeks.' 'Then, Sir,' Treves is supposed to have replied, 'You will go as a corpse.' So the necessary arrangements were made, on 24 June 1902 the new king – sixty years old, obese, a heavy smoker: 'all the risk factors' – had his appendix abscess drained two days before the planned coronation, and the ceremony ultimately took place on 9 August. Treves (who, it appears, already had 1000 operations for appendicitis to his name) became a baronet – and his arms gained an augmentation of honour, a lion of England in chief. And as Harold Ellis, that charming historian of surgery, remarks: 'this royal operation did much to draw the general public's attention to the disease'.[7]

What it did not do, however, was impart a sense of urgency to the medical profession as a whole. As early as 1914 David (later Sir David) Wilkie of Edinburgh had described the dangers of acute obstructive appendicitis and the need for early operation; yet fifteen years later Heneage (later Sir Heneage) Ogilvie would be driven to lament the progressive increase in mortality that still occurred with each day that operation was delayed – from 5.9% on day 1 to 33% on day 6 – an analysis that suggests delay was still normal enough practice, at least in London, to have provided the data on which he reported.[8]

Even in the 1920s, the management of appendicitis had only comparatively recently become the province of the surgeon. In the 1922 edition of *An index of differential diagnosis of main symptoms*, the section on right iliac fossa pain [i.e. pain in the right lower quadrant of the abdomen] was written, not by a surgeon but by the principal author, Herbert French, physician to Guy's and the Royal Household.

Moreover, that durable surgical text, Rose and Carless's *A manual of surgery*, thought it proper as late as 1937 to begin its section on the treatment of appendicitis thus:

> **Formerly perityphlitis was the exclusive property of the physician, but nowadays appendicitis is more justly within the realm of the surgeon; at any rate, a surgeon should**

13 Sir Frederick Treves [detail of the cartoon by Spy, in *Vanity Fair*] did much to bring the surgical treatment of appendicitis into favour, and was rewarded with a 'lion of England' as an augmentation of honour to his arms.

always share the responsibility of treatment with the physician, since at any moment complications may develop even in cases which appear to be simple, when immediate surgical assistance will alone hold out any chance of saving the patient.[9]

The delays implicit in such a circumspect approach would account for the policy, advocated in 1920 in an earlier edition of Rose and Carless and appropriate for a late case, of packing the appendix cavity and treating the area with bipp [bismuth, iodoform and paraffin paste, a much-respected dressing for contaminated wounds in its time].

Churchill's appendicectomy was carried out after consultations on 16 October between Lord Dawson, Sir Crisp English and Dr Hartigan, (but only after the lapse of a further day, such was the measured pace of surgical intervention in 1922). Sir Crisp was the operating surgeon, Hartigan his assistant; the anaesthetic (open ether) was administered by Dr Chaldecot. The appendix was black and gangrenous from its tip back to its origin from the caecum; it had perforated at its mid-point and was removed with some difficulty, a wound drain being inserted. Two weeks after the operation English reported to Dawson that the sutures had been removed, and the wound was dry except where the drain had been; the patient had been up that day for the first time. English had been impressed by his patient's 'surprising powers of recuperation'; he was progressing at about fifty percent more than the normal rate, and had expressed a desire to travel to Dundee for a campaign meeting ten days later.[10]

14 Churchill's own operation, twenty years after Treves had brought respectability to the procedure, was performed by Sir Crisp English.

* * *

Churchill was unable to get to Dundee until the final week of the campaign – Clemmie deputised for him until then, though it was less than two months since the birth of their daughter Mary; on the platform she received her share of abuse. When he did arrive, he was gaunt and weary, still with his wound not fully healed.

15 The 1922 election, in which Churchill lost his seat, was an unhappy episode. He underwent his appendicectomy on the night that the Tories decided to break up the wartime Coalition; Clemmie deputised for him until he was able to travel north himself, his wound still unhealed.

Arriving on 11 November he was determined to attend the Armistice Day parade, but had to be 'frog-marched' on to the parade [a]; he was then carried on an improvised 'sedan-chair' to the hall where he was to address a meeting [b]; obliged to sit while speaking, he is as gaunt about the face and jaw as at any time of his life [c].

Certainly his had been no easy procedure and, as he recorded later, his wound was seven inches [18cms] long. Arrived in Dundee, he needed to be supported on each side, was obliged to sit to speak, and was heckled incessantly. One heckler predicted Churchill would be at the bottom of the poll: he was not far wrong.

So Churchill found himself without his appendix, without a portfolio, without even a seat. His support came from unexpected quarters: as he left Dundee by train after his defeat, he was seen off by a party of amiable students, one of whom – an Irishman – called out 'Collins believed in you, we believe in you.' But it was not, by and large, a happy situation, even though he was made a Companion of Honour that year.

He tried for a couple of years, working his way back towards the Conservatives, before re-entering parliament in the safe seat of Epping (elected as a Constitutionalist, he shortly rejoined the party that had earlier treated him so shabbily), to become Chancellor of the Exchequer in Baldwin's Cabinet – he had emulated his father in this, and had retrieved his career by the end of his fifth decade.

Table 5

THE FIFTH DECADE 1914-24

Influenza

Widespread bruising (crash landing in aircraft)

Abrasions to hand (thrown by camel)

Appendicitis (pre-election appendicectomy)

- and various 'near-misses' on active service

16 Churchill became Chancellor of the Exchequer in 1924, thus emulating his father (whose robes he wore with pride during the presentation of five Budgets).

NOTES

1   Gilbert [2004] p.337.

2   History – and in particular folk-history – has not been kind to Churchill in the matter of Gallipoli. It has chosen to assume that he directed the enterprise in detail, as well as conceiving it in outline: whereas, in Montgomery's words, 'a brilliant strategic idea had been thrown away because of every conceivable mistake in its execution by the commanders' [Montgomery, BL (1968) *A history of warfare* (1968): London: Collins. p.487] Seldom has an inspired idea been more perverted in the execution, or more distorted in the recollection: in 2005 an otherwise intelligent man told me that he 'could never forgive Churchill for sending Kiwis to be slaughtered there, as if they were [expendable] colonial levies'. In fact it was Kitchener who directed the land campaign, and who sent Anzacs on the grounds that – as he explained to the Cabinet – first class [i.e. British] troops were not needed to fight the Turks. Loyal Antipodeans would assert that the Anzacs did not do a bad job.

3   The evacuation was skilfully handled by General Sir Charles Monro, who had succeeded Hamilton as commander-in-chief; it is a curious coincidence that he should have been a grandson of Alexander Monro *tertius*, for three generations of Alexander Monros occupied the chair of anatomy in Edinburgh University for over a century (from the appointment of Alexander *primus* at the age of 22 in 1719 to the welcome retirement of Alexander *tertius*, the weakest member of the dynasty, in 1836). The Monros are a phenomenon in medical history, and not without significance in military history as well. Churchill, however, found it hard to accept Monro's role, commenting bitterly in *The World Crisis*, [p. II: 388] 'General Monro was an officer of swift decision. He came, he saw, he capitulated.'

4   When he reported himself to the Guards battalion which was to acquaint him with the niceties of trench warfare, the commanding officer broke the silence of his welcome by observing, 'I think I ought to tell you that we were not at all consulted in the matter of your coming to join us.' The regiment was to make amends: it was a bearer party of the 2nd Battalion, The Grenadier Guards, that bore Churchill's coffin into St Paul's Cathedral on 30 January 1965.

5   Gilbert [2004] p.392.

6   Lawrence, TE: *Seven Pillars of Wisdom*. 1962; Harmondsworth, Penguin. [first published 1926] p.283n.

7   Ellis, H: *History of Surgery*. 2001: London, Greenwich Medical Media. p.114.

8   Macintyre, IMC: Personal communication, 2007. Wilkie's paper was published in the British Medical Journal [1914: 2: 959]; in 1930 he expressed his satisfaction that surgeons were increasingly heeding his earlier call for early operation [*Can Med Assoc J*; 1930, 22: 314] Macintyre comments: 'I suspect that he was referring to practice as he had seen it in Edinburgh and North America!'

9   Wakeley CPG & Hunter JB (eds) *Rose & Carless Manual of Surgery*. 1937; London: Baillière, Tindall and Cox. p.1223.

10 Churchill's operation notes and associated papers are in the Churchill Archives Centre in Cambridge [WCHL 6/64]. They document the lasting friendship that developed between Churchill and his surgeon. In September 1939, when Churchill had once again become First Lord, English must have written congratulating him: a telegram of acknowledgment reads 'thank you so much'. And in 1942, a week before Alamein as it happens, English wrote again, recollecting that it was then 'exactly 20 years since I had the honour of doing the operation on you for acute appendicitis'. His notes, he went on, 'remind me of the great severity of the attack... and the splendid way in which you defeated it.'

VI

THE LOCUST YEARS

Sir Thomas Inskip…
who was well versed in the Bible,
used the expressive phrase
about this dismal period…
'The years that the locust hath eaten'
– Joel ii.25.

- WSC: *The Second World War*, I: 52n. (1948)

For five years Churchill delivered Budgets that built his reputation as a resolute if controversial Chancellor;[1] but disagreements with his Conservative colleagues on subjects such as Protection and India freshened up old hatreds, and then in 1929 Labour won a general election and Ramsay MacDonald formed what shortly became a cross-party government. Out of office but with his popularity as a speaker guaranteed in North America, Churchill resorted to a trans-Atlantic lecture tour, travelling in company with his brother Jack, his son Randolph and Jack's son Johnny: they called themselves 'the Churchill troupe' but it became almost a royal progress.[2] On the day of his return to New York the stock market crashed.

17 The Churchill Troupe – Winston and his brother Jack, with their sons Randolph and Johnny, travelled to Canada in the liner *Empress* of Australia, formerly *Tirpitz* and intended as the Kaiser's yacht.

Within a year Churchill had split with the Tories over India, and in 1931, no longer a member of Baldwin's Shadow Cabinet and deprived by the 1929 crash of much of his investment income, he again travelled to the US for a lecture tour as a fund-raising measure.[3] In New York in December 1931, looking the wrong way after paying off a taxi, he was struck by an approaching car. The impact, on his forehead and thighs, was severe enough to put him in hospital for a week, where he had the added misfortune of developing pleurisy. He also acquired a scar to which Best draws attention in his text, describing the tour as 'financially successful but marred by an accident in New York which left him with a scar on his forehead'. It left him with more than that.[4]

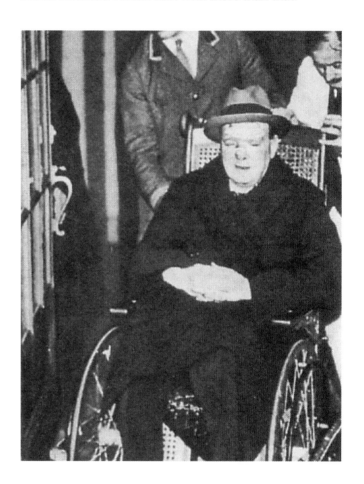

18 Churchill still looked rather the worse for wear when he left Lenox Hill Hospital in New York in December 1931 after his encounter with Mario Contasino's car.

Writing later, of his recollections of the impact, Churchill noted that

> There was one moment – I cannot measure it in time – of a world aglare, of a man aghast. I certainly thought quickly enough to achieve the idea '*I am going to be run down and probably killed.*' Then came the blow.

I felt it on my forehead and across the thighs. But besides the blow there was an impact, a shock, a concussion indescribably violent. It blotted out everything except thought...

I do not understand why I was not broken like an egg-shell or squashed like a gooseberry.[5]

After a couple of weeks more convalescing in New York (amusing himself by calculating the force of the impact, with the help of his scientific friend Professor Lindemann),[6] he went to the Bahamas, impatient, depressed and suffering pain in the arms and shoulders which I consider to have originated in his cervical spine.

In this belief I am supported by another of his published accounts (this one in the *Daily Mail* of 29 December 1931). He emphasised that he was not even briefly unconscious, but that when he tried to move his limbs, 'neither hands nor feet took the slightest notice' so that he began to fear 'some serious injury to the spine';

'then violent pins and needles in both my upper arms and... fingers beginning to move in accordance with my will. Almost immediately after, the toes responded to my orders... Blood continued to flow freely from my forehead and nose ...

Such loss of motor power in all four limbs, even brief as his was, suggests that his cervical spine was given 'a good fright', and with it the spinal cord at that level.

Spinal injury centres are full of young men whose willingness to dive into what proves to be shallow water has rendered them tetraplegic.[7] Churchill was fortunate that the neck injury which rendered him temporarily unable to move his arms or legs did not produce more lasting and total disability. What it does provide, however, is an explanation for the recurring neck and shoulder symptoms he would suffer.

In his record of his 'Encounters with Winston Churchill' the neurologist Lord Brain has described the x-ray appearance of Churchill's cervical spine in old age:

Gross changes: marked lordosis from the 1st to the 5th cervical vertebrae, while the 5th, 6th and 7th were kyphotic; their bodies appeared fused together, C5 and C6 at an angle leading to the kyphosis,

with wide separation of the tips of the spinous processes of these two vertebrae, apparently due to old trauma.[8]

[Lordosis is the spinal curve, convex forwards, which at a lower level produces sway back; kyphosis, on the other hand, is concave forward and produces a 'round back'. The neck vertebrae should be aligned in a gentle lordosis – a kyphosis such as described here is evidence of substantial damage.] The 'old trauma', Brain conjectures, was the 1893 fall from the young spruce tree. If so, (and I believe it was so: we should bear in mind that as early as 1899 the Boers' 'Wanted' notice referred to Churchill as 'walking with a forward stoop', which would suggest a neck deformity) the degenerative process between then and 1931 will have made Churchill vulnerable to the effect of further neck injuries; and the 1931 injury will in turn have accelerated the degenerative process.

* * *

19 The scar of Churchill's New York accident of 1931 is well displayed in this detail from the celebrated photographic study by Karsh of Ottawa. The full portrait appears as the frontispiece of this book.

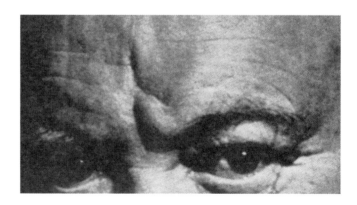

The blow on his forehead, forceful enough to lead to a substantial scar, would have forced his head backwards (and his neck into hyperextension, as the movement is called) and it is this movement, with an element of forced rotation of the neck – again credible, since his scar was not quite in the midline – that represents the classic form of what has been called 'whiplash', the neck injury that more commonly occurs among vehicle *occupants*, and from a rear-end shunt. As MacNab defined it about forty years ago, the extent of the damage depends on the fact that, whereas the neck can be hyperextended some way with the head in the midline, the range available diminishes sharply when the neck joints are 'locked' by being rotated at the time of impact.[9]

In litigious countries, the label 'whiplash', once it became widely employed, provided the basis for prolonged disability and large settlements among those who suffered a neck injury; when New Zealand moved to a scheme of no-fault accident compensation in 1974, the incidence and cost of whiplash diminished dramatically. But 'classic' whiplash, meeting MacNab's criteria in respect of the biomechanics of the impact, was – and remains – a major injury. It is not surprising that Churchill went sore and despondent to the Bahamas.

His recovery must have been helped by the income from his published account of the accident. Written in dramatic prose, this served not only for publicity (which he did not commonly shun) but to recoup the loss of lecturing income that resulted from his period of incapacity. When he returned to London in March 1932, his friends met him with the gift of a Daimler car (which must, in itself, have been therapeutic, if the benefit achieved by successful whiplash plaintiffs in later years is anything to go by.).[10]

At this stage he had completed his history of the Great War, and was starting on a biography of his celebrated ancestor John Churchill, 1st Duke of Marlborough. This took him in September 1932 to the field of Blenheim, but a planned holiday in Venice was prevented when he developed paratyphoid fever.

* * *

The group of infections once known as 'enteric fever', later distinguished as deriving from the typhoid and paratyphoid A, B and C varieties of *Salmonella* organisms, had an evil reputation, and during the South African War enteric fever was both prevalent and commonly lethal. The situation in Egypt and Gallipoli in 1915 was not greatly better, but thereafter vaccination (commonly with the triple vaccine TAB – that is to say, formulated to protect against typhoid and the A and B varieties of paratyphoid) brought the problem among fighting troops very largely under control.

Under control, indeed; but not eliminated. And in peacetime, among populations not enjoying even the temporary immunity conferred by vaccination, two manifestations of infection by typhoid and its relatives continued to exercise students of public health. The first was that the organisms could be spread through contaminated water or milk, or by food either washed in infected water or handled by infected fingers. The second, sometimes even more worrying, was that such contamination could be spread by a symptomless carrier of the disease, someone who continued to excrete the causative organisms and, if employed in food handling, could bring about a local outbreak. Churchill, writing to his cousin Sunny (the 9th Duke of Marlborough) when he first returned to England, gave it as his opinion that 'it was an English bug which I took abroad with me and no blame rests on the otherwise misguided continent of Europe.'[11] In this view he may himself have been misguided.

He was indeed something of an infidel in matters of immunisation and the like. As far back as his departure for South Africa in 1899 'private reasoning had led him to refuse inoculation for enteric fever on the voyage out'[12]; and only stern lobbying by Lord Moran ahead of Churchill's midsummer visit to Italy in 1944 could persuade his patient to defer to expert advice and 'take mepacrin as a safeguard against malaria'.[13]

* * *

Churchill had a couple of weeks in a sanatorium in Salzburg, but his condition relapsed after he got home at the end of the month, and there he bled profusely from a paratyphoid ulcer. This relapse, on 27 September 1932, was typical of the course of the disease which, after an initial period of headache and general malaise (sometimes with clouding of consciousness: the name 'typhoid' was culled from the Greek *typhos*, a cloud), makes its attack on the lymphoid tissue of the lower part of the small intestine, producing ulcers which may either bleed profusely or even perforate the bowel wall.

The management of substantial blood loss was not, in the early 1930s, a straightforward matter. Regeneration of blood cells is a slow process, which may occupy several weeks; and blood transfusion as a 'routine' procedure was in its infancy between the wars, though the first attempts at transfusion dated back as far as the seventeenth century.

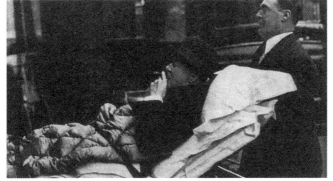

Richard Lower [1631-91] transfused blood between animals, and this led to efforts to transfuse blood from animal to man – with the prospect of a disastrous outcome. Not until 1900, when Landsteiner [1868-1943] identified the ABO pattern of blood groups, could human transfusion achieve a rational basis; in 1914 the ability of citrate, added to donor blood, to inhibit clotting was recognised and the 'window of opportunity' for carrying out the procedure was widened. But it remained a tedious procedure and its use in civilian practice was minimal until after the Second War had prompted the development of 'blood banks'. Even in 1948 Handfield-Jones and Porritt could write (though this view may have survived from an earlier edition of their book)

20 For someone who has recently been close to exsanguination from a bleeding paratyphoid ulcer, Churchill is looking remarkably chirpy as he leaves a London nursing home on 10 October 1932.

> **The latter [blood transfusion] is obviously the method of choice, but certain technical difficulties and certain possible sequelae make it applicable only under favourable conditions... The first essential is to find a prospective donor whose blood is safely miscible with that of the patient.[14]**

No mention of obtaining blood from a bank or transfusion service. In the therapeutic climate of the

1930s, Churchill's recovery was necessarily a tedious business.

He missed the Tory conference in Blackpool in October, and was still too weak to travel up to London from Chartwell (his home in Kent) when, in early November, the House discussed disarmament in the face of the ominous rise of the Nazi party.

It also served, that relapse, to prevent his attendance at a dinner celebrating George Harrap, his publisher, on the 50th anniversary of his entry into the firm. Asked by the younger Harrap to contribute a message to be read out at the event, he offered, 'every good wish to Mr Harrap on this occasion, in the hope that his future as a publisher will not be unworthy of a long and distinguished past.' But his illness did not prevent him from maintaining the traffic in MS pages, proofs and the like, as he pursued the career of his ancestor the first Duke.

* * *

By the end of the month Churchill was fit enough to speak a warning that, if Britain forced France to disarm, Germany (with her numerical superiority) would seek revenge for her 1918 defeat. It was not a message his colleagues wanted to hear. They would not listen for the next seven years - years that, for Churchill, have been called 'The Wilderness Years'.[15]

Churchill himself called them 'The Locust Years' in a chapter title in his history of the Second War. There a footnote credits Sir Thomas Inskip with having used the term.[16] It was Inskip, a nonentity, who held the post – of Minister for the Coordination of Defence - that should have gone to Churchill. Inskip's two main claims to fame appear to have been his propensity for losing the legal cases entrusted to him, and the regularity with which he reneged at bridge.

Sir Philip Gibbs, who wrote perceptively of the British character, was a member of a Royal Commission set up, under the chairmanship of Sir John Eldon Bankes, to look into alleged abuses in the private manufacture of arms and trading in weapons of war. He describes the reception of the Commission's Report by the House of Commons.

Sir Thomas Inskip rose, and ... professed that he did not understand some part of our recommendations, and that anyhow the Government had appointed some experts to elucidate them. Considering the utter

simplicity of our plan and prose, it does not say much for the intellectual ability of Cabinet Ministers and their advisers. Sir Thomas Inskip did not like the Report, it seemed, and damned it with faint praise, and sent it to its grave.[17]

Gibbs had had occasion to visit Churchill at Chartwell during these Locust years. He described how he had

.... wanted to have a talk with a man... whose career – with all its faults and all its failures – will be written in history also as that of the most brilliant and dynamic figure of our time. [18]

He brought secret information on Britain's unpreparedness, and was encouraged if surprised to find that Churchill's network of informants had already provided this material. What must strike us, however, is the opinion of Churchill that he brought along with his information; for these words, written in 1937, would have been astounding and far from universally acceptable to Gibbs' reading public. If we bear in mind that Gibbs had pacifist leanings in the 1930s (at their meeting that day, Churchill had laughingly dubbed him 'a goody-goody') this judgment on a man 'in eclipse' must impress us as prescient,

Remarkably, Churchill's health seems to have been good, even if his spirits received one blow after another, through these years of frustration; as first MacDonald (with Tory backing), then after 1935 Baldwin, and ultimately Neville Chamberlain sought to suppress him and his warnings by fair means or (more often) foul.

Table 6

THE SIXTH DECADE 1924-34

Head and thigh injuries (motor vehicle accident) with brief tetraparesis

Subsequent pleurisy

Brachalgia (cervical spine injury in vehicle accident)

Recurrence of depression

Paratyphoid

NOTES

1   The most controversial decision was to return Britain to the Gold Standard, a move that Churchill inherited from his predecessor as Chancellor, and towards which he was urged by Treasury officials. Changing circumstances altered the merits of the measure and J M Keynes, enlisted by Churchill to help persuade them against the move, produced a critical pamphlet entitled *The economic consequences of Mr Churchill*. For seventy years popular opinion branded Churchill a fiscal incompetent; but recent studies tend to rehabilitate him. The subject is dealt with in vol. 5 of Gilbert's official biography [chapters 4-14; and its accompanying Companion Volume *The Exchequer Years*]. To rehabilitate Churchill from an established Churchill myth is never easy.

2   The travellers described themselves as 'the Churchill Troupe', and they travelled in the Canadian Pacific liner *Empress of Australia*, which had begun life as *Tirpitz*, laid down in 1913 for the Hamburg-Amerika line. Her building was suspended at the outbreak of the war, until in 1916 the Kaiser, scenting victory, had her completed to serve as a Royal yacht in which he could receive the surrender of the British fleet. She became part of the reparations package after the Armistice. I am sure Churchill relished the pedigree of the vessel that transported the Churchill Troupe. But it is worth recording that *Empress of Australia* did achieve her destiny as a Royal yacht, when in 1939 she carried King George VI and Queen Elizabeth to Canada just prior to the outbreak of the next war.

3   On this occasion, Parliamentary business forced Churchill to defer his sailing, and the only available substitute booking was in a German liner, *Europa*. She and her sister ship *Bremen* had snatched the Blue Riband from the old *Mauretania* in 1930.

4   Best, G: *Churchill: a study in greatness*. 2001; London, Hambledon & London. [Paperback edition, Penguin: 2002; see p.130.] So far as can be determined from a study of photographs, including Best's paperback cover, the scar resembles a 'k', of which the stem merges into the crease that leads to the inner end of the left eyebrow. The Karsh detail emphasises the vertical and lower oblique limbs of the 'k'.

5   Quoted in Broad, L: *Winston Churchill 1874-1952*. 1952; London: Hutchinson. p. xiii.

6   Lindemann became Lord Cherwell in 1941. His Germanic family name, as Best points out, is misleading (though his personality was Teutonic in some of its elements). His father left Alsace after it fell under German occupation following the Franco-Prussian War of 1870 – though he remained a German citizen until 1904, before becoming naturalised so that young Frederick would not be liable to military service in the German army. 'The Prof' himself was born in England (of a Russian-American mother) and grew up with a dislike of Germany. He was professor of experimental physics at Oxford, and blessed with the ability to explain complex scientific matters in lay terms.

Churchill's cabled request reads:

Please calculate for me following What is impact or shock to stationary body weighing two hundred pounds of motor car weighing two thousand four hundred pounds traveling [*sic* – either Churchill was learning American spelling quite rapidly, or the Western Union clerk improved on his 'Limey' version of the word] thirty or thirtyfive miles per hour [stop] This shock I took in my body being carried forward on the cowcatcher until brakes eventually stopped car when I dropped off Brakes did not operate till car hit me [stop] Want figure for article Think it must be impressive Kindly cable weekend letter at my expense [this instruction refers to the practice by which long cables were transmitted at a cheaper rate at weekends] Am expecting recover completely in month Pretty good Your friend Winston.

The original was delivered in typed capitals; punctuation varied between the insertion, twice only, of the word 'stop', and the use of a double-space (which, in this 21st-century rendering, has prompted the computer to recommence with a capital letter).

Six days later, Lindemann's reply (from the Hotel Continental, Nice) reads:

Just received wire delighted good news [stop] Collision equivalent falling thirty feet onto pavement equal sixthousand footpounds energy equivalent stopping ten pound brick dropped sixhundred feet or two charges buckshot pointblank range [stop] shock

presumably proportional rate energy transferred [stop] Rate inversely proportional thickness surrounding skeleton and give of frame [stop] If assume average one inch your body transferred during impact at rate eight thousand horsepower [stop] Congratulations on preparing suitable cushion and skill in taking bump Greetings to all

In his biography Lewis Broad duly quotes the calculated impact as 'the equivalent of falling thirty feet on to a pavement.' But he then describes Churchill's injuries in dramatic terms: 'His injuries were grave. Fifteen bones were broken, there was internal haemorrhage and for two days life itself was in danger.' Packwood's essay in *Churchill and the Great Republic* is more restrained: 'Churchill was left bleeding, shocked and badly bruised, but no bones were broken.' (Clementine, telegraphing to young Randolph, recorded 'two cracked ribs'.) From Packwood we learn that 'a receipt for $250 for "professional services rendered" during December 1931 by Dr Foster Kennedy survives among' the Churchill papers.

It is interesting that the forces involved in this injury approximate those that Churchill survived in 1893 when he fell from the young spruce tree.

7   Tetraplegia: paralysis of all four limbs; also known as 'quadriplegia' by those who do not mind mixing Latin and Greek etymology. Tetraparesis denotes temporary, as opposed to established, paralysis.

8   Russell Brain [later Lord Brain, 1895-1966] saw Churchill in consultation with Lord Moran in 1949 and on a number of occasions thereafter. His account of these consultations appeared in 2000 (with an introduction by his son, Michael C Brain) in *Medical History*: 44: 3-20. It is an illuminating and fascinating account by the man who happens to have succeeded Moran as president of the Royal College of Physicians of London.

9   Ian MacNab was an English expatriate who became a prominent orthopaedic surgeon in Toronto; his account of 'Acceleration injuries of the cervical spine' was published [p.1797] in the proceedings of a symposium on disease and trauma of the cervical spine sponsored by the American Academy of Orthopaedic Surgeons and published in the *Journal of Bone & Joint Surgery* [46A: 1765-1821] in 1964.

10 There were eight donors: Lord Burnham (proprietor of the *Daily Telegraph*), Sir Harry Goschen (chairman of Churchill's Epping constituency committee), Esmond Harmsworth (son of Lord Rothermere, proprietor of *The Times*), Lord Lloyd (recently returned from a posting as British High Commissioner to Egypt), Lord Londonderry (Churchill's second cousin, Lord Privy Seal at this time), Sir Harry McGowan (Churchill's financial advisor, chairman of ICI), Sir Archibald Sinclair (Liberal MP and shortly leader of the party, Secretary for Scotland, Churchill's 2i/c in France) and the ever-loyal Brendan Bracken (who was journalist, financier and politician in his time). It is an interesting group, gathering together so many of Churchill's own interests.

11 Gilbert [2004] p.590.

12 Guedalla, p.81. The only 'statistic' that I carry in my head about the South African War and 'enteric fever' derives from my history of the local (Antipodean) Wellington College's involvement in that war: of five deaths among serving Old Boys, all but one were from typhoid. As Churchill himself said, 'Life is a whole, and luck is a whole' – and here (as so often) in deciding against inoculation, he was lucky.

13 Moran, p. 162. In his account Moran cites the evidence he marshalled; and on this occasion, I am on his side.

14 Handfield-Jones, RM & Porritt, AE: *The essentials of modern surgery*. 3rd edn 1948; Edinburgh: Livingstone. pp. 149-50.

15 Gilbert, M: *Winston Churchill: the wilderness years*. 1981; London: Macmillan.

16 Churchill, WS: *The Second World War: I – The gathering Storm*. 1948; London: Cassell. p. 52n.

17 Gibbs, P: *Ordeal in England*. 1937; London, Heinemann. p. 85-6.

18 *Ibid*. p. 332.

VII

STIRRING AND INSPIRING

The one really stirring and inspiring speech on the progress of the present war was made by Mr Winston Churchill, who is one of the few men in parliament who are also genuine men of letters.

- Dorothy L Sayers, *Begin here*, 1939.

The wilful blindness of the Tory 'leadership' continued. Baldwin even explained his dishonest behaviour at the time of the 1935 election to Churchill in these terms:

> **Supposing I had gone to the country and said that Germany was rearming and we must rearm, does anybody think... this... democracy would have rallied... at that moment? I cannot think of anything that would have made the loss of the election... more certain.**[1]

Chamberlain, for his part, had seen Churchill as a rival for years; so when he succeeded Baldwin he ignored Churchill's warnings, he allowed the annexation of Austria, the occupation of Czechoslovakia (in two bites, this one); he went to Munich and came back waving a piece of paper which he claimed to represent 'peace in our time'[2] – and only in September 1939, at the outbreak of war itself, when the entire country recognised that Churchill's warnings had, after all, been sound, did he invite his rival to return to the Admiralty. Even before Churchill reached the door, the message had gone out to the fleet: Winston is back.

Back into office, indeed: but it was not until Hitler's simultaneous invasion of France and the three Low Countries in 1940 that Chamberlain bowed to the inevitable and Churchill at last became Prime Minister, on 10 May 1940. He was also presented, at the urging of his Cabinet (and on the initiative of Lord Beaverbrook or, according to Montague Browne, of that other political gadfly, Brendan Bracken), with an attendant physician: Sir Charles Wilson, who had won a Military Cross in the trenches of France in 1916, who had been an enterprising Dean of St Mary's Hospital Medical school and who would enter, the following year, on a nine-year tenure of the presidency of the Royal College of Physicians of London.

To the world Churchill presented an image of resolution which – in part because it contrasted so starkly with what had gone before – inspired his countrymen; but to his friends and colleagues he showed the grimness of his mood to such a degree that Clementine composed a letter to him, explaining

> **There is a danger of your becoming generally disliked by your colleagues & subordinates because of your rough sarcastic & overbearing manner... my darling Winston – I confess that I have noticed a deterioration in your manner; & you are not so kind as you used to be.**[3]

Having written thus, she tore up the letter; four days later she rewrote it and handed it to her husband. But six months later, on Churchill's 66th birthday, Eden could write to his boss:

> **Very few men in history have had to bear such a burden as you have carried in the last six months. It is really wonderful that at the end of it you are fitter & more vigorous, and better able than ever to guide & inspire us all.**[4]

The contrast between these two letters serves to highlight the strains of the 'settling-in' process that Churchill had to undergo. He had, after all, inherited a disaster; he enjoyed few resources apart from his own personality and oratory with which to avoid utter defeat. Yet during the second half of 1940 he had succeeded in convincing his people that victory was possible. That was no small achievement, and one which, for the most part, did nothing but emphasise the greatness of the man. But he was not totally free of human frailty.

21 'Practice and perseverance are alone necessary,' he had told his mother after his visit to Semon about his speech defect. Churchill's oratory, defect and all, inspired his people throughout the war. This was his triumphant broadcast, on 8 May 1945, in which he announced victory in Europe.

* * *

About the middle of this six-month period occurred an incident which both portrays the stresses under which Churchill was then operating, and represents the start of one of the few instances when Churchill's generosity of spirit briefly deserted him. General Sir Archibald Wavell had been appointed in July 1939 to set up Middle East Command, and had embarked on a process of making bricks with very little straw. When Italy entered the war, the territory she held in north-east Africa (where she had swallowed Ethiopia [Abyssinia] in 1936) extended in continuity between Eritrea and Italian Somaliland. This, combined with her presence in Libya, sandwiched the British forces in Egypt in ominous fashion. The Ethiopean swallow had also isolated French and British Somaliland from the rest of Africa.

Despite the complications introduced by France's surrender, Wavell's forces succeeded in driving the Italians out of Cyrenaica at the end of 1940, and out of East Africa by May 1941, before the division of resources – which became necessary in order to assist Greece in 1941 – led to a succession of disasters: Greece itself was lost, then Crete and (with the advent of Rommel to North Africa) all the gains lately achieved there as well. At this point Wavell was transferred to India, to exchange jobs with Auchinleck (who would in turn share Wavell's fate, in August 1942).

In August 1940, Wavell had been called home for consultations. At this stage of the East African campaign, the Italians were threatening British Somaliland, and Wavell had given permission to his 'locum' as commander, Maitland Wilson, to decide whether to hold or evacuate the country. He declined to overrule this permission when urged by Churchill to hold the place at all costs, believing that lives mattered more (given his shortage of manpower) than territory.

By the time he got back, the country had indeed been evacuated. The low casualty rate [the historian Liddell Hart gives a figure of 'barely 250'[5]] prompted Churchill to direct an angry signal to Wavell accusing him of not having fulfilled his undertaking that the place would at least be fought for. By the time this signal arrived, the extent of the Italian casualties became known: attacking with a preponderance of five to one, they had lost 1,800 men [indeed Liddell Hart says 'over 2000']. In replying to the Prime Minister's signal Wavell pointed this out; and added the unfortunate sentence: "Heavy butcher's bill not necessarily indication of good tactics." This remark so annoyed Churchill that, when Eden and Sir John Dill (then Chief of the Imperial General Staff) visited Wavell in Cairo in April 1941, Wavell and Dill

discussed in the car Wavell's relations with Churchill; and Dill said: "I don't think he will ever forgive you for that last sentence in your signal about Somaliland.[6]

In Churchill's history of the Second War, the matter of casualties sustained and inflicted is glossed over, and all his emphasis is on the fact that the evacuation of British Somaliland 'remains on record as our only defeat at Italian hands'.[7] Even during Wavell's visit to London, which laid the foundations for this contretemps, Churchill had been critical of his general, telling Eden that Wavell 'was a good average colonel', who would make a 'good chairman of a Tory association'. 'I do not feel in him that sense of mental vigour and resolve to overcome obstacles, which is indispensable to successful war,' he wrote to Eden, who responded, 'Dill and I were much perturbed at your judgment of Wavell.'[8] Given Churchill's opinion of Wavell prior to the unfortunate signal, the effect of the signal itself becomes understandable, if regrettable.

Thus, although Wavell and his PM could exchange biblical telegrams after the Cyrenaica offensive of December 1940,[9] their relationship was already poisoned. And I wonder how much this poisoned relationship (and the sense of 'walking on eggshells' that Wavell was amply sensitive enough to have felt) serves to account for his subsequent readiness to send forces into Greece without real demur, readiness which forms the basis of much of de Guingand's 'critical reassessment' of Wavell.[10] The whole episode, however, does serve to underline the effect on Churchill of the stresses imposed on him by the situation he had inherited; for, in easier times, he and Wavell might at least have built on their common devotion to poetry – Churchill, it will be recalled, won a school prize for reciting a massive portion of the *Lays of Ancient Rome*, while Wavell built, out of his own capacious memory, one of the better anthologies of English verse, *Other Men's Flowers*.

* * *

As Britain stood alone, though, and saw off the threat of invasion in the summer of 1940, Churchill had come to embody the spirit of the British people. His oratory belied, indeed could exploit, his speech defect. 'This was,' he told his listeners, 'their finest hour' – in a way it was also his.[11]

In 1941 he stood amid the ruins of his beloved House of Commons, and resolved to see it rebuilt – which it was, with seating limited enough (at his insistence) to produce a crowded chamber on big occasions. And though 1941 offered little of consequence in the way of victories, it did bring the two enemy blunders that would make the war winnable.

In June, Hitler's invasion of Russia mobilised the massed strength of a country driven by an ideology as fierce as Hitler's own; and six months later Japan's attack on Pearl Harbor (followed four days later by Germany's declaration of war against the US) brought that country into the war. Both events had prompt transatlantic consequences for Churchill.

On 9 August, some six weeks after Hitler's invasion of Russia, and with Stalin already demanding military help from Britain, Churchill and the American president, Franklin D Roosevelt, met in Placentia Bay in Newfoundland and established a blueprint for the world then and the world to come, predicated (somewhat paradoxically) on the US remaining at peace. Usefully in the circumstances, the US agreed to give aid to Russia in coordination with Britain and 'on a gigantic scale'.

Churchill's preparations for the meeting were complicated by the development of an abscess at the root of his right upper canine tooth, for which he was seen by Wilfred Fish. Later Sir Wilfred and a significant figure in the development of dentistry in his century, Fish had cared for Churchill's dental needs over a number of years. In the early Chartwell days, when Fish was practising nearby in Sevenoaks, he performed an emergency repair on Churchill's upper partial denture, which broke on the Friday of a weekend leading up to a speech in the House on the Monday. Some time later, in 1936, he dealt with Churchill's request for a 'right angle dental syringe' which would allow him to wash out a cavity in a back tooth. The 1941 emergency was even more challenging: conventional root canal work would have involved repeated attendances over several days; Churchill did not have several days to spare. Fish's solution was to drive a red-hot needle into the root of the tooth, leaving the abscess free to drain over the period of the Newfoundland voyage. (No doubt some form of anaesthetic was employed.) At a later stage the tooth was extracted and a substitute added to Churchill's partial denture which is now in the possession of the Royal College of Surgeons of England, as an example of elegant gold dental work.[12]

* * *

Three weeks after Pearl Harbor Churchill crossed the Atlantic again, this time to visit the US to plan Allied strategy with his friend Roosevelt. In Washington he addressed a joint session of the two Houses of Congress. 'I cannot help reflecting,' he told them, 'that if my father had been American and my mother British, instead of the other way round, I might have got here on my own.' They loved it; though they loved far less Churchill's blunt historical account of America's failure to involve itself in Europe in time to avert the catastrophe.[13]

22a,b A tablet in the National Cathedral in Washington DC bears an extract from Churchill's speech to Congress on 26 December 1941, just before his first heart attack which occurred that night

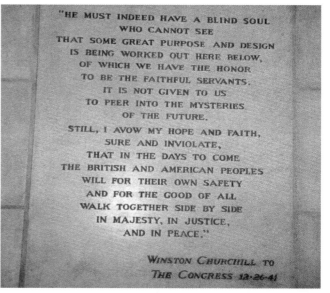

"HE MUST INDEED HAVE A BLIND SOUL
WHO CANNOT SEE
THAT SOME GREAT PURPOSE AND DESIGN
IS BEING WORKED OUT HERE BELOW,
OF WHICH WE HAVE THE HONOR
TO BE THE FAITHFUL SERVANTS.
IT IS NOT GIVEN TO US
TO PEER INTO THE MYSTERIES
OF THE FUTURE.
STILL, I AVOW MY HOPE AND FAITH,
SURE AND INVIOLATE,
THAT IN THE DAYS TO COME
THE BRITISH AND AMERICAN PEOPLES
WILL FOR THEIR OWN SAFETY
AND FOR THE GOOD OF ALL
WALK TOGETHER SIDE BY SIDE
IN MAJESTY, IN JUSTICE,
AND IN PEACE."

WINSTON CHURCHILL TO
THE CONGRESS 12·26·41

Washington Cathedral   South Elevation

But this visit was to be the occasion of his next medical adventure. He was staying at the White House, and got up in the middle of a hot night to try to open a window.

> **It was very stiff (he told his physician Charles Wilson). I had to use considerable force and I noticed all at once that I was short of breath. I had a dull pain over my heart. It went down my left arm.**[14]

He had suffered his first heart attack. The accepted six weeks of bed rest for a coronary thrombosis in those days was out of the question, for political reasons as well as because of the patient's temperament. 'You mustn't do more than you can help in the way of exertion for a little while', Wilson told him. It was therapy years ahead of its time.

* * *

The management of heart disorders has been a challenge, their understanding elusive, over a couple of centuries. Credit for the first description of angina is given to William Heberden [1710-1801], a Cambridge graduate who practised in London and became physician to George III. In his *Commentaries*, written in 1768 for the guidance of his son and namesake, though not published until the year after his death, he described how

> **Those who are afflicted with it, are seized while they are walking (more especially if it be uphill, and soon after eating) with a painful and most disagreeable sensation in the breast, which seems as if it could extinguish life, if it were to increase or to continue; but the moment they stand still, all this uneasiness vanishes... The pain... very frequently extends from the breast to the middle of the left arm.**

Heberden recognised the disorder as progressive; he wrote

> **After it has continued a year or more, it will not cease so instantaneously upon standing still; and it will come on not only when the persons are walking, but when they are lying down, especially if they lie on the left**

side... The termination of the angina pectoris is remarkable. For if no accident intervene, but the disease go on to its height, the patients all suddenly fall down, and perish almost immediately.

Edward Jenner (best known for having initiated vaccination for smallpox) corresponded with Heberden on the subject,[15] having recognised – as Heberden had failed to do – that this cardiac pain resulted from coronary artery disease. 'How much the heart must suffer,' he wrote, 'from the coronary arteries not being able to perform their functions I need not enlarge upon'. From Berkeley in Gloucestershire, Jenner also corresponded with his Bath colleague Caleb Parry, whose 1799 text on angina advanced well-documented opinions with due acknowledgment to Jenner. But the coronary artery-cardiac pain link would not be universally accepted for a century or more.

We have to feel sorry for Jenner. His old chief, John Hunter, suffered his own first coronary thrombosis in 1772, his next in 1776 (when he was 'extremely ill' and took himself to Bath to convalesce). There was a further attack in 1777, which once again prompted Hunter to travel to Bath; Jenner came to see him there, but out of consideration did not enlarge on his views to Hunter as he had done to Heberden. Hunter lived until 1793, his life being (as he described it) 'at the mercy of any rogue' who cared to anger him – which indeed suggests that he was more aware of his situation than Jenner was prepared to make him – and, at autopsy, was found by his brother-in-law Everard Home (another former pupil) to have coronary arteries in an advanced state of disease. 'The coronary arteries,' Home reported to Jenner, 'had their branches... in the state of bony tubes which were with difficulty divided with the knife.'

For many years no integrated understanding of coronary heart disease was achieved. In the journal *The Practitioner* for July 1968 (the centenary of its founding) Sir Ian Hill, a past-president of the Royal College of Physicians of Edinburgh, describing the evolution of cardiology, noted that it was Herrick, in 1912 and 1916, who first described myocardial infarction [the destruction of heart muscle from blockage of its blood supply] as a clinical entity. He went on to recall that

In Mackenzie's book on 'Angina Pectoris', published in 1925, whilst there are case histories characteristic of myocardial infarction, neither that term nor coronary thrombosis is even mentioned. The first

cases described in this country were in 1926 by McNee and again by Carey Coombs, and I personally saw my first patient with myocardial infarction as a house physician in 1928. The diagnosis was made by a young clinical tutor, A. Rae Gilchrist, and the condition was one of which neither my Chief nor I had ever heard.

By the time of Churchill's first coronary attack the link with cardiac pain was well enough understood, but the management of the condition was, then and for some while after, exceedingly cautious. The articles in the second volume of *Refresher Course for general practitioners* were first published in 1951-52; there, in his essay on the subject, that erstwhile clinical tutor, A. Rae Gilchrist, by now Reader in clinical cardiology in the University of Edinburgh, recommended a week to ten days of bed rest for an episode of coronary insufficiency, but for a frank coronary thrombosis contended that

Rest in bed must usually be maintained for six weeks or thereabouts, and the more complete the inactivity during the first three or four days the better. During this time the patient should do nothing for himself. He is to be fed and washed; visitors must be excluded and sleep ensured… Among hospital patients, treated as we believe under the best conditions, conservative measures yield a mortality rate of 33% in this country.[16]

Against protocols such as these, the boldness of Wilson's counsel – not to 'do more than you can help for a little while' – is as spectacular as its soundness in the circumstances.

* * *

Churchill returned to London in January 1942 to face a winter of discontent. Britain's first exercise in bringing naval strength to the Pacific had ended disastrously. Churchill held the new battleship *Prince of Wales* in special regard, having travelled in her – along with a number of shipwrights who were still at work when she sailed – to his Placentia Bay meeting with Roosevelt; now she and *Repulse* were caught without air cover off the Malayan coast when they sought to disrupt the Japanese landings. Both ships were sunk by Japanese aircraft, and the story was put abroad that they had been despatched without an accompanying aircraft carrier on Churchill's orders and against Admiralty advice. That canard was shot down in the course of a grumpy Commons debate on the conduct of the war at the end of the month; but in February Singapore surrendered; and the sequence of reverses continued to the point where, while revisiting the United States in June, Churchill had the embarrassment of receiving news of the fall of Tobruk and something close to a rout of the British forces in North Africa.

This time he returned to face a vote of censure in the Commons. He had to defend his record with one hand tied behind his back, in that he was unable to reveal much of the planning and activity that was going on, but his contribution was robust:

Every vote counts. If those who have assailed us are reduced to contemptible proportions and their vote of censure on the National Government is converted into a vote of censure upon its authors, make no mistake, a cheer will go up from every friend of Britain and every faithful servant of our cause, and the knell of disappointment will ring in the ears of the tyrants we are striving to overthrow.

The censure motion was lost, 25 votes to 475. But the problems of morale and command in North Africa remained.

In August 1942 Churchill elected to fly (by the roundabout route via the Mediterranean and Teheran [now Tehran]) to Moscow for his first meeting with Stalin. This journey was to be made in an American Liberator bomber, uncomfortable and unpressurised, and involved climbing to an altitude of 15,000 feet. It would therefore be necessary to use oxygen masks. Gilbert records that Churchill took himself to Farnborough to try out the mask – and have it adapted so that he could smoke his cigar while wearing it.

On the way out he called at Cairo, long enough to replace Auchinleck (who had attempted to combine the roles of commanding Eighth Army with his overall Middle East command, after Cunningham and then Ritchie 'burned out') with 'Alex' – General Alexander. For the Eighth Army itself he set out to obtain formal Cabinet backing to appoint 'Strafer' Gott, whose record to date was impressive and of whom (at a meeting in the desert) Churchill formed a high opinion.

But by the time this approval arrived Gott was dead, his aircraft shot down as he flew off on a short leave before taking up his new post. Montgomery, languishing in England where he had assembled the post-Dunkirk defences, and noted for his acerbity, was hurriedly substituted: 'If he is disagreeable to those about him,' Churchill wrote to Clementine, 'he is also disagreeable to the enemy.' On such chances can the course of history depend.

On his way back from Moscow Churchill reached Cairo in euphoric mood. Sir Alexander Cadogan noted in his diary that the Prime Minister was

> **in terrific form and had enjoyed himself like a schoolboy, having bathed twice. He held forth the whole of dinner, ragging everyone. Sir Charles Wilson, his 'Personal Physician', is one of his principal butts. To Winston's delight, poor C.W. fell ill of the usual local tummy complaint, and Winston now goes about saying to everyone 'Sir Charles has been a terrible anxiety to us the whole time, but I hope we'll get him through!' Last night at dinner Winston held forth to the whole table on medicine, psychology &c (all Sir Charles' subjects) and worked himself up to a terrific disquisition. I suspect (and I inferred from Sir Charles' expression) that it was pretty good nonsense. And I think Winston must have had an inkling of that too, as he ended up 'My God! I do have to work hard to teach that chap his job.'[17]**

In the course of this stopover Churchill visited Montgomery's headquarters and also addressed a parade of New Zealanders who had played a prominent part in denying Rommel his hoped-for conquest of Egypt. 'You have played a magnificent part,' he told them – 'a notable and even decisive part in stemming a great retreat which might have been most detrimental to the whole cause of the British Empire and the United Nations.' He was photographed by General Freyberg's PA, Captain (later Sir) John White; the photograph was suppressed by the censor, on the grounds that it made the PM look too ferocious – what the censor did not know was that the PM was screwing down the corners of his mouth in an effort to deny entry to some dozens of desert flies.

A visit to the Australians cost him dearly: the Diggers crowded round him, calling out 'Good on you, Winnie – give us a cigar'. He extended his cigar case and was soon left lamenting, 'My lovely cigars – they have taken all my lovely cigars.'

Alexander, who recalled the raid, assures his readers that the PM did not begrudge them their spoils.

23 The censor would not release this photograph of Churchill's visit to 2 NZ Div because 'it made the PM look too fierce'. What the censor did not appreciate was that Churchill was attempting to keep numerous desert flies out of his mouth. It is just possible to make out two of them.

And 1942 brought the first dividends: 'It may almost be said,' Churchill wrote later, '"Before Alamein we never had a victory. After Alamein we never had a defeat."'[18] Reporting to the Commons on 11 November (about three weeks after the beginning of the final Alamein battle, and three days after the Anglo-American North African landings) he described the terms in which he had briefed General Alexander after appointing him in August:

1. **Your paramount duty will be to attack or destroy at the earliest opportunity the German-Italian army, commanded by Field Marshal Rommel, together with all its supplies and establishments in Egypt and Libya.**

2. **You will discharge or cause to be discharged such other duties as appertain to your command without prejudice to the task described in Paragraph 1 which must be considered paramount to His Majesty's interests.**

'The general,' Churchill commented at the time, 'may very soon be sending along for further instructions.' It is possible to discern the play of emotions – pride, relief, the feeling of having been justified by events – that permeated this coda to the mid-year vote of censure.

Following the break-out at Alamein, Montgomery's Eighth Army drove westwards to take Tripoli after a frenzied couple of months, so that by the end of January 1943 Alexander (Churchill's fellow Harrovian and fellow-artist) was able to report:

> **Sir**
>
> **The orders you gave me on 15 August 1942 have been fulfilled. His Majesty's enemies together with their impedimenta have been completely eliminated from Egypt, Cyrenaica, Libya and Tripolitania. I now await your further instructions.**[19]

Further west, the slower progress of Operation Torch (the Anglo-American landings along the western rim of North Africa, which brought the name of Eisenhower to the attention of the world) demonstrated the relative inexperience of the forces involved.

Meanwhile, on 29 November 1942 Nan le Ruez, enduring life in occupied Jersey, recorded in her diary:

> **Mr Churchill was making a speech tonight. In secret John, Herbert and I heard it. I think the purpose of his speech was to keep the English from getting too elated over the victories lately. He spoke very seriously and again did not promise anything. He said 1943 would be a stern, terrible year. I felt rather depressed as I listened, but thinking it over, not so much. Mr Churchill never raises false hopes. And he knows his people, how they must always be 'kept up to it'.**[20]

It was indeed a world war: while Montgomery was hammering at Rommel, the citizens of Jersey were suffering under German occupation; and Churchill was the link that bound freedom-loving people together.

In February 1943, in the week of the capture of Tripoli, Churchill met Roosevelt at Casablanca. Mary, the youngest Churchill daughter, diaried her fear that he might suffer a further heart attack, and wondered if he should be warned off travelling; but she and her mother agreed to leave well alone. The meeting was designed to plan the conduct of the war but, within a week of his return to the English winter Churchill was laid low by a return of the pneumonia which had haunted his childhood. When a medical bulletin needed to be issued Charles Wilson (henceforth Lord Moran: 1943 was the year of his peerage) 'called in consultation Dr Geoffrey Marshall of Guy's Hospital… a genial but offhand physician', who confided to his patient that 'he called pneumonia "the old man's friend". "Pray explain," said Winston. "Oh, because it takes them off so quickly," Marshall answered unabashed.' He was soon established high in the P.M.'s favour, Moran commented.[21] From Moran's account, it appears that Churchill's temperature did not settle for a week or more – that is to say, this episode of pneumonia was managed in the traditional way with careful nursing and 'watchful expectancy' in anticipation of the 'crisis'.

'I was shocked when I saw him,' Mary Churchill wrote. 'He looked so old & tired.' Moran, on the other hand, asserted that 'we were at no time concerned about his condition' but went on to explain that

The patient himself took a more serious view of his illness. Apart from his appendix, he had never been seriously ill, and his attention was caught now by the high fever; his imagination did the rest.[21]

This remark deserves examination.

The suggestion that Churchill's appendix had been his only substantial previous ailment would admit of two explanations. Either Moran had failed to follow the most simple advice that goes to medical students concerning the taking of a history from a patient – hear first the history of the presenting complaint, then enquire into the past medical history (and it is plain, from the last eighty pages of this present narrative, just how voluminous that past history already was by 1943). For a former medical school dean that would be a shocking failure.

Or (and this seems far more credible) he wanted to throw into prominence the conditions which confronted him *after* he became Churchill's doctor, so as to emphasise his role in what his book took as its subtitle: the struggle for survival.

In either case, the observation does Moran no credit.

* * *

On 10 June 1943 (the centenary of the institution of its Fellowship) the Royal College of Surgeons of England elected Churchill an Honorary Fellow. Apart from his distinction as the nation's leader, he was *ex officio* (as First Lord of the Treasury, that is to say, as Prime Minister) a Trustee of the Hunterian Museum.

This museum is the jewel in the College's crown. It was created when John Hunter's collection of specimens was bought by the nation in the decade following Hunter's death in 1793; the care of this treasure was entrusted to the Company of Surgeons, of whose Court of Assistants – precursor of the Council – Hunter had been a member. The Company was transmuted into a Royal College largely in recognition of this new responsibility, and the care of the museum was placed in the hands of a group of Trustees, half of them *ex officio* appointees commencing with the Lord Chancellor and the First Lord of the Treasury, and the remainder distinguished persons of scientific bent. In the context of the Museum and its vicissitudes, it is worth noting that the College building was badly damaged by enemy bombing on 10 May 1941, the same night in which the House of Commons was destroyed; and many of the Hunterian specimens were lost, in spite of efforts which had been made either to disperse the collection or to provide secure storage. The task of reconstituting the Hunterian museum to reflect Hunter's principles has occupied the Royal College over sixty years.

For various reasons (at first not unconnected with the War) it was not until 1956 – on St George's Day, 23 April – that Churchill signed the Roll of Fellows at a small semi-private ceremony at the College. This took place during the presidency of Sir Harry Platt, but in the presence of Lord Webb-Johnson, who had been president in 1943 and had since 'driven' the rebuilding of the College.[22]

At the time of the award in 1943, the then Sir Alfred Webb-Johnson sent Churchill two short works of Rudyard Kipling. Webb-Johnson had been Kipling's surgeon, in succession to an earlier president of the College, Sir John Bland-Sutton. He had cared for Kipling in his final illness in 1936, and became a friend of his widow.[23] Because of the possibly controversial nature of the verses, she had declined publication, and only a few copies had been put together. At Churchill's suggestion, one copy went to President Roosevelt.

Churchill's status as a Hunterian Trustee (of which Webb-Johnson made mention when inviting him to accept the honorary Fellowship) prompted him to present to the College, in January 1944, the body of a platypus. The interest in the unique fauna

24 On St George's Day 1956 Sir Winston Churchill came to Lincoln's Inn Fields to sign the Roll of Fellows and receive his diploma as an honorary Fellow of the Royal College of Surgeons of England from the president, Sir Harry Platt. Chatting in the doorway recess with Lady Churchill is Lord Webb-Johnson, who had been president when Sir Winston became a Fellow in 1943.

of Australia that had caused John Hunter to provide a description of half a dozen Australian mammals for John White's *Journal of a voyage to New South Wales* in 1790, must have been communicated to Churchill at the time of his award. It is a tribute to his mental agility that, in the middle of a war, he was able to stow this information away and, six months later when a suitable opportunity arose, act upon it.[24]

It is apparent that he valued his association with the Royal College. After the visit in 1956, when at last he was able to sign the roll and receive his diploma, he wrote to Sir Harry Platt:

> **6 May, 1956**
>
> **My dear President,**
>
> **Thank you so much for your letter and the interesting enclosure. May I take this opportunity of telling you again how greatly complimented I am by the honour you have done me? The ceremony at the Surgeons' Hall was a most agreeable occasion.**
>
> **Yours very sincerely,**
>
> **Winston S. Churchill**
>
> **Sir Harry Platt, LL.D., M.C., M.S., F.R.C.S.**

* * *

Back in the Mediterranean at the end of 1943, to meet Roosevelt in Cairo before the Teheran conference with Stalin, Churchill was again unwell; and after he returned to Cairo in early December he was obviously sickening for what, by the time he reached Carthage, was to be another full-blown pneumonia. He was started on sulphonamides (a May & Baker product, the prototype was designated M&B 693); he went into atrial fibrillation, his heart rate becoming distressingly irregular. Brigadier Evan Bedford the cardiologist, and his chest physician colleague Lt-Col Guy Scadding were summoned from Cairo for consultation. Clementine came out to be with him; in his bed he was briefed on the preparations for the Anzio landings. Harold Macmillan, his Minister in North Africa, wrote in his diary:

> **At last a Colonel Buttle – the great M&B specialist – arrived from Italy. He is an expert on how to give the stuff. He seems clever, determined, rather gauche and rude – just the chap we need. I begged him to be strong and _forbid_ telegrams or visitors.**[25]

25 [From left]: Brig Evan Bedford and Lt Col Guy Scadding were whisked in from Cairo, and Lt Col G A H Buttle, 'the great M & B expert', from Italy to advise on management of Churchill's pneumonia and atrial fibrillation at Carthage in December 1943.

Just the chap we need. – Macmillan was quite right in his assessment of Buttle's worth. Lindsay Rogers was a New Zealand surgeon who wangled a posting to join Tito's partisans at the end of the North African campaign; in his account of this experience he wrote of the help he received from Lt-Col Buttle before leaving on his odyssey:

Every desert surgeon knew Buttle and his den in the cellar of the 15th Scottish. He was a man whose efforts far surpassed ours in the field; for by his efforts and his organisation more lives were saved than by any group of surgeons, and the blood he collected at No 5 Transfusion Unit poured back life into many thousands of soldiers... He was a grand chap... and ever ready to come to the front and see us at work, and advise us on the new antibiotic drugs he brought with him... Buttle as usual came to the rescue [before we left for Yugoslavia] and slipped in many a little thing for us, and gave us a good supply of the sulphonamide drugs.[26]

26 Convalescent in Carthage, Churchill celebrated Christmas 1943 with a meeting with Eisenhower and Alexander, followed by a family Christmas dinner – in his siren suit and dressing gown!

Ten days after Buttle had prescribed for him Churchill conferred with Eisenhower, then hosted an extended family Christmas dinner - in his dressing gown. As well as Clementine, Randolph and Sarah were present; so were the physicians, Moran and Bedford. In one of his happier utterances, Randolph proposed a toast:

Ladies and gentlemen, let us rise and drink to my father's health and his remarkable recovery, which is entirely due (turning first to Lord Moran and then to Dr Bedford) to M & B.

By then Buttle was probably back in 'his den'; otherwise Randolph might have gone further, to acknowledge M & 2 Bs.[27]

* * *

The development of atrial fibrillation during that attack of pneumonia is worth noting as an indication of the combined effect of Churchill's existing cardiac impairment and the further insult to his heart. The human heart has four chambers, two atria into which blood enters: venous blood from all parts of the body into the right atrium, freshly oxygenated blood returning from the lungs, into the left. Just as in a semidetached house, the right and left halves of the heart have a dividing wall which is designed to be impermeable. Each atrium, having collected its quota of entering blood, is designed to contract so as to force its contents into the corresponding ventricle; and almost immediately that ventricle is designed to contract its thicker and more powerful muscular walls so as to impel the blood onwards – to the lungs for oxygenation on the right side, and into the aorta, for distribution of oxygenated blood round the body, in the case of the left ventricle.

The heart muscle itself is nourished by way of the coronary arteries (so-called because they form a 'crown' for the heart) and depends, for its efficiency as a pump, on their remaining open. In Churchill's case the 1941 heart attack had compromised a portion of this supply.

When the heart muscle (and the nerve bundles that 'drive' its contractions) become sufficiently damaged, the atria, instead of squeezing their contents out with one confident contraction, flicker repeatedly and somewhat ineffectually; the effect is to part-fill the corresponding ventricle which, when it in turn contracts, has only a small amount of blood to discharge. Some of these ventricular contractions cannot even produce a palpable pulse at the wrist. The distressingly irregular heartbeat of his first episode of fibrillation was described by Churchill to Moran: 'My heart is doing something funny – it feels to be bumping all over the place.'[28]

As an exercise in inefficient pumping, fibrillation would be hard to beat; but its additional down-side is that the blood which bobbles about in the atrium instead of being kept moving has a fair prospect of clotting. And clots loose in the circulation are, of course, emboli which, if they originate in the left heart, are liable to lodge in the brain (causing a stroke) or elsewhere in the body.

Concerning the Carthage episode Moran records that he 'had taken the precaution... to send to Tunis for digitalis, and now... gave it to him... It was four hours before the heart resumed its normal rhythm.'[28] Digitalis, the active principle in the foxglove, was found by Withering as long ago as 1785 to 'steady' the action of the heart, and it became the mainstay of treatment of heart disorders in the days before synthetic (and more precisely targeted) drugs became available. Given Churchill's history of coronary heart disease, and given Moran's concerns about his patient's heart (as conveyed to Brooke more than once when they were travelling overseas)[29] I am inclined to the view that Moran might with advantage have been better prepared than to have 'to send to Tunis for digitalis'.

Certainly Moran sweated blood when the Cabinet back in London began to suggest he might have anyone that he cared to name, sent out to consult with him. Properly enough he saw no merit in the proposition that Churchill might be 'treated by a committee', and indeed he confided that Scadding had been brought over 'to placate the Cabinet'. But he foresaw the possibility that, in the event of an unfavourable outcome, he might have his career blighted as did Sir Morell Mackenzie when his failure to diagnose the throat cancer of Frederick, the German Crown Prince was exposed in the most spectacular possible way.

Even now, after sixty years, (he mused to his diary) the way he mishandled the illness of the Crown Prince Frederick makes a best-seller in which his infirmities, moral and intellectual, are all carefully set forth.[30]

* * *

Apart from his record of Churchill's fibrillation during this attack of pneumonia, (including a second episode on 17 December, three days after the original one had prompted him to 'send to Tunis' for digitalis) Lord Moran's writings describe an event on 20 December, during Churchill's convalescence when, as he records it,

> **The PM... is very difficult – on two occasions he got quite out of hand... He has been savaging Bedford and Scadding, who know their job and have been helpful... When Bedford, speaking impressively, advised him to rest for a fortnight, Winston suddenly became red in the face with rage... 'Have you,' he said angrily, 'in the course of your long experience ever seen a patient get a second attack of pneumonia through getting about too early?'... I was upset by Winston's rough handling of my colleagues, and when he turned to me with some asperity, without any warning my patience gave out... I told him that he must not shout at me; that he was behaving foolishly. I left him before I said more.[31]**

Fifty years later, Scadding broke silence to explain that

> **I did not keep a diary of these events, but I am sure that I should not have forgotten the experience of being 'savaged' by Churchill. My recollection is that the conversation recorded by Moran did occur, but without the emotional overtones. Moran's account of it seems to me to be unfair to Churchill, representing him as being discourteously overbearing. Like many patients with heavy responsibilities, he demanded to be told the evidence on which we gave this advice, and Bedford and I made the usual replies, in which Moran supported us; but the suggestion that he had to rescue us from Churchill's rage must be, to say the least, exaggerated.[32]**

* * *

The illness in North Africa was a sobering experience for Churchill. Back home from Marrakech at the beginning of March 1944, he told his guests he had not long to live. A couple of months later, his equanimity restored, he hosted a conference of Commonwealth Prime Ministers which attempted to reach a consensus on post-war planning. The New Zealand prime minister, Peter Fraser, who broke his homeward journey to visit his country's division in front of Cassino, returned home with a signed photograph of Churchill that is still to be seen at Parliament House in Wellington.[33]

27 The New Zealand prime minister, Peter Fraser, is escorted by General Freyberg round the ruins of Cassino on his visit to the New Zealand Division. Fraser went on to London, returning with a signed portrait as a memento of his discussions with Churchill.

Churchill's recent apprehensions about his health did not prevent him from seeking to join the armada which supported the June landings of Operation 'Overlord': it required a direct prohibition from the King himself to dissuade him; and he managed a day in Normandy just six days after the June 6 landings.

In July, after these Normandy landings had brought the first relief to mainland Europe (while, at home, flying bomb attacks reached a peak) Admiral Cunningham the First Sea Lord noted one night: 'very tired and too much alcohol,' while Eden wrote of 'a deplorable evening'. But Churchill managed to work late that night: 'PM in mellow mood and quite chatty for him... loads of work and got to bed finally at 3.40am,' his secretary recorded.

The following month, however, flying back from a visit to Alexander's headquarters in Rome, he succumbed to pneumonia again. Cunningham saw him that night too, and wrote, this time more sympathetically:

With all his faults (& he is the most infuriating man) he has done a great job for the country, & beside there is no one else.'[34]

And, although it takes us a few weeks out of this seventh Churchill decade, it is worth recording here (as further evidence of Churchill's ability to keep matters of detail in the back of his mind while remaining focused on the war itself) a slightly later meeting between the two men. Cunningham records a meeting of the War Cabinet with the Chiefs of Staff on 12 December 1944, a fortnight after Churchill's seventieth birthday, which

> **did not break up until 1.30 a.m., and as we were leaving the Prime Minister called me alone into the Cabinet room. He first asked if I was of Scottish ancestry, which I was easily able to confirm. He then said he had been looking into the precedence of the various Orders of Knighthood, and asked if I knew anything about the Order of the Thistle... He then said it was his intention to recommend to His Majesty that I should be created a Knight of the Thistle. It was so unexpected that I was rather at a loss for words; but realising that the honour was even more a compliment to the Navy... I thanked him warmly... Mr Churchill was obviously dead tired... I begged him to stop work and go to bed. But he would not.[35]**

Table 7

THE SEVENTH DECADE 1934-44

Coronary thrombosis

Pneumonia (3 attacks)

Atrial fibrillation (complicating pneumonia)

Violent diarrhoea (Moscow, 1944)

NOTES

1   Guedalla, P: *Mr Churchill – a portrait*. 1941; London: Hodder & Stoughton. p. 261.

2   Even the phrase 'peace in our time' lacked originality: it was the title of a book of speeches 'on England and the Empire' by Neville Chamberlain's half-brother Austen, published in 1928.

3   Gilbert [2004]: p.768.

4   *Ibid*. p.792.

5   Liddell Hart, BH: *History of the Second World War*. 1970; London: Cassell. p. 124.

6   Fergusson, BE: Wavell: *Portrait of a Soldier*. 1961; London: Collins. pp. 52-3.

7   Churchill, W S: *The Second World War*. 1949 : II: 383.

8   Gilbert, M: *Winston S Churchill*. 1983; London: Cassell. VI: 731-2.

9   The exchange is recorded in Churchill's *The Second World War* [II: 543]:

Prime Minister to General Wavell   18.xii.40
    St. Matthew, chapter vii, verse 7.
"Ask, and it shall be given you; seek, and ye shall find; knock, and it shall be opened unto you."

General Wavell to Prime Minister   19.xii.40
    St. James, chapter I, verse 17.
"Every good gift and every perfect gift is from above, and cometh down from the Father of lights, with whom is no variableness, neither shadow of turning."

When his sacking occurred in 1941 Wavell was quite free from overt resentment. His biographer, Bernard Fergusson, describes how

A signal from the Prime Minister telling him that Auchinleck and he were to change places had arrived in the small hours of the morning, and been taken to General Arthur Smith, who had at once dressed and gone round to Wavell's house on Gezira. He found him shaving, with his face covered with lather and his razor poised. He read out the signal. Wavell showed no emotion. He merely said: "The Prime Minister's quite right. This job wants a new eye and a new hand."; and went on shaving. [Fergusson, B: *Wavell: portrait of a soldier*. 1961; London: Collins. p. 59]

10 De Guingand's criticism is contained in *Generals at War* [1964; London: Hodder & Stoughton] in which he finds fault with much of Wavell's performance in 1941. 'Freddie' de Guingand was Montgomery's chief of staff in 8th Army; he managed to fall out with many of his colleagues, and I am inclined to discount his strictures on Wavell.

11 On 18 June 1940, Churchill exhorted the House of Commons in these words:
Let us therefore brace ourselves to our duty and so bear ourselves that, if the British Commonwealth and Empire lasts for a thousand years, men will still say: 'This was their finest hour.'

The words 'this was' came out, in the slightly crackly recording of the period, as 'Thish wozh…'

12 Manson, J D; *Wilfred Fish and a profession in the making*. 2003; London: Esmeralda Press.

13 Gilbert, M: *Churchill and America*. 2005; London: Simon & Schuster. p.249. Had Hitler not declared war on the U S four days after Pearl Harbor, it could be argued, the American response could well have been to concentrate its involvement in the Pacific, as Admiral King and others urged.

14 Moran [1966]: p. 16. 'I had no doubt… that his symptoms were those of coronary insufficiency,' Moran goes on to observe. 'The textbook treatment for this is at least six weeks in bed. That would mean publishing to the world – and the American newspapers would see to this – that the P.M. was an invalid with a crippled heart and a doubtful future. And this at a time when America has just come into the war, and there is no one but Winston to take her by the hand.' It was an appalling dilemma that Wilson had to confront; and whatever one's opinion of his later behaviour, one must applaud his courage in this situation.

In *Churchill and America* [2005; London: Simon & Schuster, p.250] Martin Gilbert gives credence to the suggestion by Mather: 'that the pain was no more than a muscle strain, or a strain of the body [*sic*, for 'bony'] and cartilaginous chest wall. This may actually be more likely, since there were no apparent adverse effects on Churchill.' It may be noted that Churchill had speculated in the same vein at the time of his attack: Moran (then still Sir Charles Wilson) recorded his patient's hopeful observation, 'My idea is that I strained one of my chest muscles.' Obituary columns are sprinkled with the names of those who have dismissed their chest pain as due simply to indigestion or 'a muscle strain'.

15 Jenner had been a favourite pupil of John Hunter, and indeed turned down an invitation to sail as naturalist on Cook's second voyage, in order to enter general practice in Berkeley in Gloucestershire, and there to pioneer cowpox inoculation for smallpox. It is one of history's little coincidences that, on the *Endeavour* voyage, Cook and Banks were entertained at Madeira, their first port call, by William Heberden's brother Thomas, who was physician to a substantial expatriate British community. He had recently died when Cook – without Banks this time, and of course without Jenner – called again at the beginning of the second voyage.

16 Gilchrist, AR: Coronary artery disease, in *Refresher course for general practitioners; 2nd collection*. 1954: London; BMA. pp. 136-7. Gilchrist would become president of the Royal College of Physicians of Edinburgh 1957-60.

17 David Dilks (ed.) *The diaries of Sir Alexander Cadogan 1938-1945*. 1971; London: Cassell. p. 475.

18 Churchill, W.S: *The Second World War*. 1951; IV: 541.

19 *Ibid*. pp. 644-5.

20 Quoted in *The Assassin's Cloak* (ed. Taylor, I & E; 2003: Edinburgh, Canongate.) p. 582.

21 Moran; C McM Wilson, Lord: *Winston Churchill; the struggle for survival 1940-1965*. 1966; London, Heron Books p.88.

22 Admission to the Honorary Fellowship of Sir Winston Churchill, KG. *Ann. Roy. Coll. Surg. Engl*. 1956; 18: 339.
    In Memoriam: Sir Winston Churchill KG OM PC. *Ann. Roy. Coll. Surg. Engl*. 1965; 36: 129.
    The originator of a method of repairing a recurrent dislocation of the shoulder, Sir Harry Platt (the first orthopaedic surgeon to be president of the English Royal College) doubtless felt that it was too late, in this instance, to offer orthopaedic advice when admitting Sir Winston to the fellowship.

23 It was on Webb-Johnson's advice that Mrs Kipling gave her husband's collection of medical history volumes (including a number written by Bland-Sutton) to the fledgling Royal Australasian College of Surgeons. These form an interesting segment in the College's rather splendid historical library; they are referred to in my paper *A web of words*, published in 1999 [*Aust NZ J Surg* 69:252]

24 John Hunter (1728-93) was the leading surgeon in London in his time, and has been described, on his tomb in Westminster Abbey, as 'the founder of scientific surgery'. He amassed a collection of over 13,000 specimens to document his view of the inter-relationship of structure and function in living things and, after his death, these were secured for the nation and entrusted to the Company of Surgeons (which became a Royal College in recognition of this responsibility). James Cook, also born in 1728 and to become Hunter's friend, brought back specimens for him; so did Joseph Banks, who catalysed the friendship of the two older men. When the First Fleet arrived in Sydney in 1788, the surgeon-general, John White, gathered specimens of six Australian mammals (five of them

marsupials) and offered them to Hunter, publishing Hunter's description as an appendix to his *Journal*. Churchill was in good company in his gift of the platypus.

25 Macmillan, H: *War Diaries*. 1984; London: Macmillan. p.327. Of this occasion Moran wrote [p. 150]: 'Harold Macmillan is inclined to fuss. As the only Cabinet minister here, he claims that all decisions ought to be submitted to him. But this is a medical matter; and any decisions that have to be made are going to be made by me and no one else. Bedford has just arrived from Cairo... his presence here will keep the people at home quiet.' Macmillan, for his part, recorded in his diary that 'Moran seems very worried. He is telegraphing all over the place for specialists.' I do not think there was too much mutual respect here.

26 Rogers, L: *Guerilla Surgeon*. 1957; London: Collins. p. 16ff.

27 Lewis Broad, in his biography of Churchill [1952, p.479] attributes the wording of this toast to Winston himself.

28 Moran [1966]: p. 151.

29 Bryant, A: *The turn of the tide*. 1957; London: Collins. This book is based on quotations from the [genuine, in his case] diaries of General Sir Alan Brooke (later Viscount Alanbrooke), CIGS and chairman of the Chiefs of Staff Committee – which is to say, the PM's chief military adviser in both the purely army and the tri-service sense. These items are printed along with Brooke's 'notes on my life' which expand the diary entries, and a somewhat adulatory commentary by Bryant. When the touring party reached Cairo on the way to Moscow in August 1942, Brooke recorded: '[The PM] has got his doctor with him who tells me he was a little worried about his pulse.' [p.438] And on their return, when problems arose with the timing of the North African landings, and the need to hold face-to-face discussions with the Americans was being discussed, the Brooke diary goes on: 'Sir Charles Wilson asked to see me. He told me he had heard that P.M. was thinking of going over to America... He said that last time the P.M. was in Washington he had trouble with his heart and he thought it unwise for him to go.' [p. 493] Plainly Wilson fretted – reasonably enough – about his patient's

cardiac outlook; he may well have felt that his management of the 1941 coronary had bordered on the cavalier; but one might expect such concerns to translate into better preparedness, for in those days digitalis and quinidine were about the total armamentarium for the management of disorders of heart rhythm, and to carry a supply of one or the other 'in his purse' would have been a wise precaution, as well as reassurance to himself.

30 Moran [1966] p. 152. A footnote describes how 'in 1887 [Mackenzie] was summoned to attend Crown Prince Frederick William of Germany. The Crown Prince, who became Emperor Frederick William III in the same year, died of cancer in 1888. Mackenzie had ruled out this diagnosis when he was called in.' Sir Felix Semon, who had advised the young Churchill concerning his speech defect, played a part in the subsequent humiliation of Mackenzie.

31 Moran [1966] p. 153-4.

32 Scadding, JG [1993] A summons to Carthage, December 1943. *BMJ*: 307: 1595. Scadding describes the whole episode of his visit in charming terms, even to pointing out gently that Moran is in error in the timing of his arrival. (Moran defined Scadding's summons thus: 'To placate the Cabinet, I had asked the people in Cairo to send him.' I think Moran enjoyed his ability to conjure up experts whenever it pleased him.)

33 Churchill and Fraser got on well, meeting frequently on Fraser's numerous visits to London during the war. A note made by Col [later Lt-Gen Sir] Ian Jacob in 1941, and quoted by Hensley, G [2009; *Beyond the battlefield: New Zealand and its Allies 1939-45*], reads: '"That dear old man", as the Prime Minister calls Mr Fraser... is as honest and straightforward as you make them.' Perhaps Churchill chose not to recognise that he himself was ten years older than Fraser.

34 Gilbert [2004]: p.905.

35 Cunningham, A B: *A sailor's odyssey*. 1951; London: Hutchinson. p.622-3. Cunningham notes that he 'could remember no naval officer outside the Royal Family who had ever received this great distinction'.

VIII

IRON
CURTAIN

An iron curtain is drawn
down upon their front.

- WSC to President Truman, 12 May 1945[1]

By the final year of the war, Churchill was a tired man: this is not surprising, given the continued pressures he had endured since 1940. In his study of these years, Max Hastings tells of the occasion when

> **Smuts told Eden after a lunch of the prime minister's: 'He may be mentally the man he was, he may be, but he certainly is not physically. I fear he overestimates his strength and he will wear himself out if he is not careful.' The wise old South African took care to say this within earshot of the prime minister. Ismay was wryly amused by the sternness with which Smuts often urged on Churchill the care of his health, admonishing him for overstaying his bedtime. The prime minister responded 'rather like a small boy being sent off by his mother'.[2]**

As it happens Field-Marshal Smuts was a mere four years older than Churchill, but the wise counsel he provided on a regular basis was rather that of a father-figure than of a near-contemporary. It was to become even more valuable.

The Yalta conference in early 1945 was the one at which Roosevelt's paranoia about British imperialism prompted him into a furtive alliance with Stalin, a compact that prevented a drive from Italy into the centre of Europe and laid the foundations for the Cold War. It was a trying conference for Churchill, forced to watch Roosevelt in decay – a dying man, immune to logic and wavering in viewpoint – and finding himself relegated to the position of odd man out; but he rose to the challenge and, though outmanoeuvred on the handling of Poland's borders, did gain some safeguards for Greece.

28a,b There is a fanciful likeness between the group photograph of the Big Three at Yalta, and the sculpture group [here shown mirror-image] which decorates the lawn at Churchill College.

Learning late in the conference, in a signal from Montgomery, of the breaching of the Siegfried Line, Churchill was in good form. 'PM seems well,' wrote Sir Alexander Cadogan, the Foreign Office mandarin, 'though drinking buckets of Caucasian champagne which would undermine the health of any ordinary man.' (It may have been intended as prophylaxis against a recurrence of the violent attack of diarrhoea that beset him on a Moscow visit the previous October. In any case it is proper to note that Gilbert, his biographer, gathered the assurances of men who worked closely with Churchill – Colville, Peck, Buchan-Hepburn who became Lord Hailes – that Churchill drank highly-diluted whisky, and less champagne than gossip claimed.)[3]

By May 1945 Germany was beaten, but Churchill himself was seriously affected by the strain of achieving this victory. At this time Peter Townsend was equerry to King George VI; recalling the prime minister's weekly visits to Buckingham Palace, for lunch, he wrote:

> **George VI paid a special compliment to his veteran prime minister on these Tuesday visits. Normally the King's equerry met the King's visitor at the door and conducted him to the King's study. But when Churchill came to lunch, the King came to the door himself, waiting for him at the top of a short flight of steps... I was there when Churchill came for one of his last luncheons. He was bowed with weariness and the King watched anxiously from the top of the stairs as Churchill mounted them, advancing the same foot at each step and unsteadily dragging the other after it. The King-Emperor, proffering his hand, almost hauled Churchill up the last two steps.[4]**

Churchill sought to prolong the wartime coalition until Japan was beaten, but was obliged to go to a general election, which the Labour party won in a landslide. It seemed that his political career was at an end, but he carried on as Leader of the Opposition (and indeed leader of the party that had treated him so shabbily during the years of appeasement).

He was grateful when Alexander (now Field Marshal, commander-in-chief in the Mediterranean theatre, and presiding over a region at peace) offered him a holiday in the villa on Lake Como which had become Alex's private retreat. He flew out at the beginning of September 1945, in the prime ministerial aircraft which

Attlee, his successor, had placed at his disposal. He was able to indulge the passion for painting which had first come to his rescue in the aftermath of Gallipoli and was now to do so in another period of rejection. 'It may be a blessing in disguise,' Clementine had told him as the election results came in. 'At the moment it seems quite effectively disguised,' was his reply.

But with his easel and the peace of Lake Como his equanimity could return: after his second painting day he told his daughter Sarah, 'I have had a happy day.' To her mother Sarah reported, 'I haven't heard that for I don't know how long.'

Alex joined him after a few days, and they painted together. Alexander was an artist of ability and friendly with the painter Edward Seago, who made his own comparison of the two men:

> **The amateur is somebody who is very often pleased with something he's done. The professional is always disappointed. Churchill, to my mind, was the amateur of all amateurs. He thought he could do it, and he did it. He never explored; he never questioned; he never observed. He painted a house if it were there, and if it had a red roof, right, here's the red paint; if there was a green field beneath it, right, here's the green paint. It never occurred to him to ask how red is the red, how green is the green, and by putting the green against the red, does the red look brighter or turn the green grey? This never entered his head. But with Alex it did all the time.[5]**

Seago's strictures on Churchill's unsubtle approach are perhaps unduly harsh. Sir John Lavery, whose standing as an artist was at least equal to Seago's, assessed Churchill's ability in his memoirs:

> **I know few amateur wielders of the brush with a keener sense of light and colour, or a surer grasp of the essentials. I am able to prove this from experience. We have often stood up to the same motif, and in spite of my trained eye and knowledge of possible difficulties, he with his characteristic fearlessness and freedom from convention, has time and again shown me how to do things. Had he chosen painting instead of statesmanship, I believe he would have been a great master with the brush.[6]**

* * *

Churchill's time at Lake Como was punctuated by the appearance of a hernia, for which he was seen by Brigadier Harold Edwards, who was summoned from Alex's headquarters. Edwards wrote a detailed account of his meeting with Churchill, and later summarised the circumstances:

> **On Sept 3rd I had a message – an urgent call to go to Como to see Churchill, which came from Lord Moran. A Fairchild plane was put at my disposal. We reached Milan early afternoon on the 4th, having refuelled in Rome. The journey had taken seven hours and throughout it I had been in a fever heat of anxiety as to what I might find. I was under the impression that Churchill was seriously ill. Arrived at the house I was met by Lord Moran, who told me that Churchill was out painting. What a relief! What had happened was that Churchill had suddenly developed an inguinal hernia. After examining the patient I was subjected to a detailed examination which would have done credit to an examiner for the FRCS.**

Harold Edwards' son, Professor AWF Edwards, provides an interesting postscript:

> **Father used to tell the story that after he had advised Churchill against a hernia operation he went to Milan with his army technician to get a truss made. They found a surgical outfitter opposite the Cathedral and tried to order a truss for delivery the next morning. The owner said that was quite impossible. Father (a Brigadier) explained that unfortunately he would therefore have to commandeer the shop so that his technician could make the truss himself. Ah, said the owner, is it for the famous man staying on Lake Como? Then it will be ready first thing in the morning.[7]**

This truss Churchill was to wear for a couple of years, just as he had been obliged to do in childhood. Moran mentions the hernia and the truss, but glosses over Edwards' visit and the actual obtaining of the truss, which is arguably the best part of the whole episode; later [p. 319] he writes of its limitations as a means of controlling the hernia.

* * *

The New Year in 1946 brought Churchill admission to that select band, the holders of the Order of Merit. He appreciated it in part because it carried no special style or title, and he valued his status as a commoner.

He began the year with a trip to the US, travelling in *Queen Elizabeth* and then in a train provided for them which 'must have cost a fortune – not on the Govt. either this time', as his secretary, Jo Sturdee, wrote home to her family. She recorded her boss's routine on tour:

> **This morning there were 278 letters & this afternoon more still. It is just impossible because the old man dictates memoirs, telephones all over the <u>world</u>, sends telegrams ditto, & tells one to 'write nice letters' all over the shop… Mr C says I'm to put them all in a sack & forget about them as he wants me to keep myself 'fresh' (??!!) for his work. I ask you! What would you do with him? Actually they're both very very nice – touch wood – up until now. Mrs C is in high spirits & I think it's doing her good. We had an anxious day (PRIVATE) yesterday with the Old Man but he's quite better today.**

29a,b From 1945, when he was seen by Harold Edwards, Churchill wore a truss to control his inguinal hernia (as indeed he had been obliged to do in childhood).

She enclosed that letter with one dated the following day, 22 January 1946, a short note to her secretarial colleagues:

> **We had to phone Lord Moran the day before yesterday. Everything is all right now, however. He is being kept indoors for 4 days as a precaution. It wasn't his lungs though**

they feared it was at first. You might like to tell Lord Moran he is quite OK. Temperature down to normal.

The cavalcade went on to Cuba, where they learned of further shortages back home.

The Old Man is quite affected by it & spouts his propaganda about the starving population of the 'valiant – indeed triumphant – upholders of freedom.' He is a first-class Ambassador!!... According to statistics, the scale of wastage in America is one whole meal in seven. Disgusting – but jolly nice while it lasts.[8]

Free of the worst demands of domestic politics, Churchill was able to turn his attention to the matter of a stronger Europe during 1946.

Speaking on 19 September at the University of Zurich, he promised to 'astonish' his audience, and his proposal for 'a kind of United States of Europe' did not disappoint, for he listed two ambitions that were surprising in the circumstances of the time: 'The first step in the re-creation of the European family,' he told them, 'must be a partnership between France and Germany'. And he went on, to assert that to avoid global destruction it was necessary for Britain and the Commonwealth, as well as 'mighty America, and I trust Russia' to become reconciled; 'for then indeed all would be well.'[9]

30a,b Churchill's Zurich address of 19 September 1946 is commemorated in this plaque outside the guildhall.

Let into the pavement outside the Zurich guildhall is a plaque which records this prescient challenge. It reads: EUROPE ARISE : STEH AUF EUROPA.

* * *

Churchill had his share of further ailments: troublesome episodes of conjunctivitis which would worry him into old age, and an alarming cough in 1947, when he was back at Marrakech in North Africa, this time to paint and work on his war memoirs.[10] Jo Sturdee was again in the travelling party and gave a spirited account of two crises. The first was administrative:

> **Yesterday [20 December] was a hell of a day what with one thing and another… Mr C had been terribly worried because the various things (book manuscript and therefore most valuable and irreplaceable) which had been sent off from here on 15th and 16th had not arrived in London, whereas the powers that be – really the POWERS THAT BE – here had said that his papers would be in London in 24 hours. We have therefore had frantic telephone calls to Paris which have all been quite unintelligible… Mr C insisted on talking to Paris himself. We told him it would be no good he wouldn't hear them. But no, he would do it. Well he carefully bellowed his message, which could be heard all over Marrakech, and got as a reply a Horace kind of burble. He got purple in the face, his eyes bulged and then he nearly jumped out of bed in his wrath and threw the receiver to other side of the room, instrument and all. The stream of language was wonderful. Lizzie and I stood our ground and said, 'We told you so,' and persevered on our own. Such is life, and we still survive.**

And then, on 7 January 1948, writing home about 'Mr Churchill's health':

> **It was rather an awful moment (private) when his temperature went up soon after 2 one afternoon (which is the time when temperatures rise for pneumonia). However when we knew that Lord Moran was coming everyone felt better at once – and from then we haven't looked back. Life has become somewhat more complicated by the avalanche of Mrs C. Lord and Lady Moran and then hundreds and thousands of Press-Men from England, France and everywhere who came flying here in special planes galore, hoping to be in at the death, only to find the Old Fox sitting in his usual place in the dining room looking as round and as well as ever [8]**

And this time there was no pneumonia and Churchill was soon back at his easel.

* * *

He had found time meanwhile to have an operation for the repair of the hernia that had troubled him intermittently over the years. On occasions he had been obliged 'to leave important meetings so that he could lie down and reduce' its bulging contents, and since September 1945, when he was seen by Harold Edwards, he had worn a truss.

31a,b Lord Moran called on Sir Thomas Dunhill [left; portrait by Sir James Gunn] to carry out a repair of Churchill's hernia in 1947. The role of [Sir] James Paterson Ross [right] in the operation is uncertain, but was plainly significant.

In June 1947 he was referred by Moran to Sir Thomas Dunhill,[11] an expatriate Australian thyroid surgeon who had been recruited to St Bartholomew's Hospital by Professor George Gask in 1920 and had become a royal favourite after removing the Princess Royal's goitre. But Dunhill was 71, just a couple of years younger than his patient, and it was some years since his surgical practice had involved much below the neck. Accordingly Gask's successor in the Bart's chair, James Paterson Ross, had his house surgeon bring in, off the waiting list, a couple of patients who had been booked for hernia repairs. Paterson Ross performed the first, with Dunhill assisting; they then changed places and 'Dunhill started the second hernia, slowly and in rather a tense atmosphere which further degenerated when he began the repair and his third suture neatly pierced the femoral vein and the wound filled with blood' – so the house surgeon concerned would recall, years later.

Having made the referral, Moran evidently felt free to record his estimate of Dunhill's weaknesses, writing

> **Dunhill rather funks an operation on a man of [Churchill's] age and eminence. He is a simple soul, though a fine craftsman, and regards Winston with awe as the man who saved this country from defeat.**[12]

This remark (and Moran's obituary tribute to Dunhill in *The Times*) aroused the ire of Dunhill's protégé and fellow-Australian Julian Ormond (Orm) Smith – and many others; but Orm's scorn went on paper when he included a couple of papers relating to Dunhill in the booklet containing his Archibald Watson lecture, which was published in 1967, soon after his term as president of the Royal Australasian College of Surgeons. In one of these papers he wrote:

> **I suppose one must be charitable to Lord Moran, once the holder of the Gold Headed cane, and ascribe his inaccurate and irresponsible statements, indeed the tenor of the book as a whole as a result of 'Wear and Tear', which happens to be the title of one of the many unimportant papers he wrote.**

In the other, an account of Dunhill and his career, he contrasted three obituary tributes:

> **Many tributes have been paid to him. The one written by Lord Moran in the 'Times' was an affront to the memory of his distinguished life. It ends 'one who had in him, so it seemed, some of the elements of greatness'. Was ever such a qualified and reluctant tribute simply wrung from a man! There were two men, who did rise to eminence in their profession, the greatest of Dunhill's disciples. The one, Sir James Paterson Ross paid a simple, sincere and moving eulogy to him in**

delivering the Funeral Oration at St Martins-in-the-Fields. The other, Sir Geoffrey Keynes... in the first Dunhill Memorial Lecture said, '... I learnt more from him than from any other man.'[13]

Officially, Paterson Ross assisted Sir Thomas at Churchill's own operation; but folklore has it that he himself was the surgeon – certainly it was he who 'was delegated to visit [the patient] daily thereafter for his postoperative care. You never (he told one of his juniors) visited him until afternoon because he did not awake before noon.'[14] The operation was carried out on 11 June 1947, at a small nursing home in Berwick Street, off Oxford Street and quite close to Dunhill's Harley Street rooms and residence. Moran, who was present, records its duration as 'more than two hours,' and goes on to explain that

Adhesions, the legacy of the operation for appendicitis years ago, made technical difficulties... I was only an idle spectator, and I kept glancing at the anaesthetist; and when from time to time he put his hand under the white sheet to feel the pulse I wondered if everything was all right.[15]

It is the anaesthetist who does not put his hand under the sheet (or perform its modern equivalent in regular monitoring) who is to be feared. The anaesthetist on that occasion, Dr C Langton Hewer, was another member of the staff of Bart's: in correspondence after Schein and Rogers wrote an ornamental version of the operation, John E Connolly described him thus:

Always known as 'Gloomy', an excellent anaesthetist who wrote at least two good monographs, introduced Trilene as an anaesthetic agent; also endotracheal anaesthesia and intensive care to Bart's.[16]

A favourite procedure for hernia repair was that described by Bassini, in which the bulging sac, into which abdominal contents (commonly a portion of the bowel) had been forced, was first emptied of its contents by gently 'milking' them back into the abdominal cavity. The sac was then tied off at its base; and the weakness in the abdominal wall corrected by the insertion of sturdy sutures joining the inguinal ligament (the firm sinew which marks the fold of the groin) to the sheet of tissue formed by the mixture of muscle and tendon that forms the abdominal wall.

* * *

Two years later, this time in the South of France, Moran was summoned again after Churchill's right leg 'went to sleep' while he was playing cards with Beaverbrook on 28 August; then his right arm 'cramped'; next morning he had difficulty in writing – he had suffered his first stroke. He kept quiet about it at the time, and Moran in his book skips over this detail; but Lord Brain's reminiscences record that he saw Churchill in consultation with Moran on 5 October 1949, back home at Chartwell. Discussing his situation with Brain, the patient speculated on the political scene.

I have my duty. I am Leader of the Conservative Party. We don't know when the Election will come. They will keep us guessing. I may be worth a million votes to the party. I must warn you that whatever advice you give me, I mean to go on. I am not afraid to die.[17]

Brain saw him again on 15 October and 8 December. By then his neurological signs were improved, and he was looking forward to getting rid of what he described as 'government of the half-wit, by the half-wit, for the half-wit' and to the prospect of an election in February.

He suffered a TIA [transient ischaemic attack: a mini-stroke, with reversible effect on cerebral function] at the beginning of the 1950 election campaign, and this may have prompted rumours of his death which circulated a week before the end of the campaign. He was quick to respond:

I am informed from many quarters that a rumour has been put about that I died this morning. This is quite untrue… It is however a good example of the whispering campaign which has been set on foot. It would have been more artistic to keep this one for Polling Day.[18]

* * *

The term 'stroke' has replaced the more flamboyant 'apoplexy' over the past half-century: it signifies a disturbance of cerebral function deriving from some disturbance in the blood supply to the brain. In broad terms, this disturbance may be one of bleeding into an area where blood should not be 'on the loose', or a blockage of the blood flow, resulting either from clotting within the vessels that supply the brain, or from the arrival of a clot washed along from elsewhere – that is to say, an embolus.

The common basis of circulatory upset in the brain is a combination of raised blood pressure and atherosclerosis [the degenerative process which thickens the walls and narrows the calibre of blood vessels – we have seen, in earlier chapters, how John Hunter's coronary arteries were reduced to the semblance of small bony tubes]. Now it will be plain that, as the blood vessels become narrowed by this process, one of two things must needs occur: either the blood pressure must increase, or the amount of blood reaching its target will be reduced. Hence the body's dilemma: if the elevated blood pressure creates a problem, it will be one of haemorrhage; but if the brain is starved of blood by narrowing of the vessels, the prospect is a stroke of the clotting type: a cerebral thrombosis – the commoner variety, but one which is less spectacular at onset.

As for the evil effects of small emboli washing up the cerebral vessels and ultimately impacting once the vessel's branches became narrow enough: manifestly, any source of multiple emboli must be seen as threatening a stroke; and we have already seen that atrial fibrillation of the heart is a potent source of embolus formation. Churchill had been subject to this complication since as far back as 1943. It is a reasonable assumption that his TIAs such as the one prior to the 1950 election were embolic in origin; either the result of his propensity to atrial fibrillation and the embolus formation it encourages, or of fragments washed off from atheromatous plaques (patches of the fatty sludge that forms in the walls of degenerating arteries) within the lining of the carotid arteries, which feed blood to the head in general and the brain in particular. The benefits of operation, to clear out the debris from a carotid artery, especially for the relief of TIAs, were demonstrated as early as 1954 by Rob and Eastcott;[19] but it was not for several years that physicians could be persuaded to refer patients for operation.

It will be evident from all this that degenerative disease in blood vessels is a generalised condition, and that affection of the brain, the heart and the blood vessels to the limbs, occurring either in sequence or sometimes in combination, is a pattern to be expected. In Churchill's case there was a further manifestation in 1959, when he developed a gangrenous little finger tip because a tiny embolus impacted in one of the small finger arteries; fortunately the collateral circulation was enough to heal the tissues adjacent to the blackened area, which separated off three months later, revealing intact skin underneath.

* * *

When the 1950 Polling Day did come, Labour's overall majority was cut to six; and within a year there was another election. Churchill's infirmities (as recorded by Lord Moran) had increased meanwhile. Russell Brain had seen him concerning the sense of 'tightness' about his shoulders and is reported by Moran to have told him that 'the cells in his brain which received sensory messages from the shoulder were dead' – which, if a true rendering, would rate as a splendid essay in obfuscation. Certainly the date is correctly recorded: 25 May 1950; but Moran writes as if this was the first time Brain had been called upon, and chooses to overlook the fact that Brain had seen Churchill on several previous occasions.

Brain's findings, moreover, may not have been accurately reported by Moran. Brain himself noted simply:

I saw him again. His symptoms were unchanged, and there were no abnormal physical signs. I have no further record of this meeting.[20]

32a,b Sir Russell (later Lord) Brain [left], who succeeded Lord Moran as president of the Royal College of Physicians of London, saw Churchill about his neck and shoulder symptoms, and was offended by Moran's quoting (or perhaps misquoting) him in the controversial book. Sir Victor Negus [right] advised Churchill on his deafness

Certainly it is difficult to see how *dead* sensory brain cells could perceive pain; and inherently unlikely that an eminent neurologist would phrase his advice so as to suggest that this could be the case.

In her biography of her mother, Lady Soames describes how, after the publication of Moran's book, with its 'wholesale quoting' of conversations without consent, the family were outraged, and 'several [other persons] complained at this breach of confidentiality in relation to essentially private conversations: among these were Sir Russell Brain (the eminent neurologist called in by Lord Moran)'.[21]

Sir Victor Negus, likewise seen in consultation about this time, is reported by Moran to have confirmed his patient's increasing deafness, telling him what he probably knew already: that he would no longer be able to hear 'the twittering of birds and children's piping voices'.[22] Again, something may have been 'lost in translation'.

But in spite of all these problems, and however we may choose to interpret them, in October 1951 Churchill was once again to become Prime Minister with a modest but workable majority. As well as the political problems he inherited, it is likely that Lord Moran sought various forms of further recognition from him. Montague Browne lists three such, observing 'I think these stories are true': a demand to be made Minister of Health, a request to be advanced to the rank of viscount and a bid to be made Provost of Eton. But he notes, on the other hand, the 'undoubted judgment and care' that Moran lavished on his patient.[23]

Certainly Churchill's medical problems went on: another TIA in February 1952, just after the King's death brought the present Queen to the throne; his friends and advisers hoped he might choose to retire after the Coronation. But he was not done yet: Harold Nicolson noted that

He is looking white and fatty, a most unhealthy look, you would say, if he were anyone else, but somehow out of this sickly mountain comes a volcanic flash.[24]

He found it harder to wade through the mass of papers that came across his desk, but he was touched in the spring of 1953 when the new Queen persuaded him to accept the Garter; ('I took it,' he wrote to his old friend Lady Lytton, 'because it was the Queen's wish.')[25]

But then, just after the Coronation (and after dining the Italian Prime Minister, de Gasperi – when himself about to leave for Bermuda) he collapsed into a chair as he was moving to see his guests off. His daughter Mary was called by an alarmed guest; she found him 'uncertain and unhappy and very incoherent'. He had suffered another substantial stroke.

It has been suggested that an action for libel brought against him at this time by one of the by-casualties of the Auchinleck sacking in 1942, Eric Dorman-Smith, may have been a precipitating factor in this event. Certainly Churchill confessed to finding this unpleasantness, which stemmed from the account in *The Hinge of Fate*, the fourth volume of his Second War history, 'a worry and a burden'.[26]

The morning after his collapse, however, he insisted on chairing a Cabinet meeting even though, as John Colville his Secretary noted, 'his mouth was drooping badly and he found it difficult to use his left arm.' He wanted to do so again the day after, and persisted until the last minute, when Christopher Soames his son-in-law finally talked him out of it. Brain was brought in again; Moran doubted if his patient would survive the weekend.

He survived, of course. In a week he welcomed the Cabinet Secretary, Sir Norman Brook to Chartwell. He was in a wheelchair, and proclaimed his intention of standing up; he waved a couple of would-be helpers away and 'by a tremendous effort – with sweat pouring down his face – levered himself to his feet and stood upright. Having demonstrated that he could do this, he sat down again and took up his cigar. He was determined to recover.'[27]

* * *

The involvement of Churchill's face and upper limb in this second major stroke permits a tentative localisation of the site of the insult to his brain tissue. As viewed from the outer side, each cerebral hemisphere has a fanciful resemblance to a boxing glove, the thumb portion of which represents the temporal lobe of the brain. Up the major part of the glove, about the summit of its curve, is a strip of cerebral cortex tissue where the main sensory and motor functions are mediated. Nerve fibres from here cross over the midline to supply the opposite side of the body with sensation or motor power.

To use another fanciful metaphor, the relation between a site on the strip, and the part of the body it is connected to, can be likened to a gymnast hanging head down over a bar: the portion connected to the head is in the lower, outer portion of the strip; above it are the trunk and upper limb-related brain cells, while the leg-related cells drape over the summit and into the chasm between the two hemispheres.

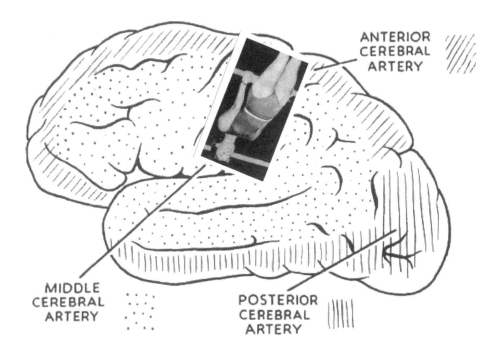

33 This diagram evolved out of an illustration drawn by the late Ray Last, who awoke a love of anatomy in the author. It is possible to see a resemblance to a boxing glove in the appearance of the brain as seen from the left side. The main areas for handling sensory and motor functions lie astride [motor in front, sensory behind] the prominent groove where a photograph of a gymnast is superimposed, whose lower limbs may be imagined hanging over the top of the brain with the lower legs hanging into the crevasse between the left and right hemispheres; the localisation of motor and sensory cells then approximates to the position of the gymnast's body parts.

The areas supplied by the main cerebral arteries are seen shaded.

The head/upper limb cells derive their blood supply from what is known as the middle cerebral artery, the lower limb cells from the anterior cerebral artery; so that a paralysis of the left side of the face and the *left* upper limb (such as was noted in Churchill's case on the morning after this second stroke, though Moran describes its onset one day later) would argue involvement of the middle cerebral artery and affection of the lower, outer portion of the so-called 'motor cortex' – on the right side of the brain.

The earlier stroke, affecting his *right* arm and leg, could on the same principle have been attributed to an insult to the left side of the brain, with the possibility of involvement of the anterior cerebral artery.

Not until the early 1970s did computed x-ray tomography [known as CT scanning] allow the production of images of affected areas – whether areas of bleeding or of damaged brain tissue – and a further decade was to elapse before magnetic resonance imaging [the MRI scan] became available to depict blocked arteries without the need for invasive injection techniques such as no octogenarian ought to suffer. At the time of Churchill's strokes, therefore, only clinical estimates of the site of his disorder could be attempted.

It is interesting to study Lord Brain's clinical notes, as gathered in the *Encounters* paper, and to admire the degree of enlightenment which clinical examination could confer.[28] Recording his findings on 3 July 1953, for instance, he observes that 'the right carotid pulse was much smaller in volume than the left' – that is to say, the blood supply to the right cerebral hemisphere, supplying portions of the brain concerned with the control of the left side of the body, was affected. It all fits together like a jigsaw; but we can also reflect that operative unblocking of the right carotid artery had just become an option, as Rob and Eastcott embarked on the series of operations that they reported the following year.[29]

* * *

Eden – though himself a sick man with a wrecked bile duct – was panting to succeed Churchill as Prime Minister; Clemmie wanted her husband to retire. But by October, fortified by the award of the Nobel Prize for literature, he returned to the Commons and produced 'an Olympian spectacle' of a speech. He then walked unaided to the smoking-room, 'flushed with pride, pleasure and triumph, sat there for two hours sipping brandy and acknowledging compliments,' as 'Chips' Channon described it. To Moran he pronounced: 'That's the last bloody hurdle; now, Charles, we can think of Moscow'[30] – for a visit to Moscow to soften up Stalin's successor Malenkov was next on his agenda. The Americans (Eisenhower was President by then, and being manipulated by his Secretary of State, the egregious John Foster Dulles)[31] frustrated his efforts.

A week before Christmas 1953 Churchill went to a lunch at Trinity House where Eden was elected an Elder Brother (a distinction that had come to Churchill himself forty years earlier). He put his lighted cigar down on his plate, rather too close to a box of matches: he suffered burns to his left hand, sufficient to demand the attentions of Moran, of Sir Thomas Dunhill once again, and then (when he repaired to Chequers) of Rainsford Mowlem, one of a quartet of New Zealand expatriates who had been among the founding fathers of British plastic and reconstructive surgery.[32]

In March 1954, after a five-hour Cabinet meeting, Moran asked if he was tired: 'Not at all.' replied Churchill; 'Now I am going out to dinner with the American Ambassador.' 'This astonishing creature,' mused Moran, 'obeys no laws, recognises no laws.' Regrettably Moran himself obeyed no conventions and recognised no responsibilities, when he elected to augment his retirement fund by a 'kiss and tell' book on his years as Churchill's medical adviser. *The Lancet* of 23 April 1966 deplored his breaking patient confidentiality in this way, as 'creating a bad precedent which none should follow'.[33] Martin Gilbert, commenting on Moran's peerage, remarks with unusual asperity, 'Churchill ennobled his doctor, Sir Charles Wilson (created Lord Moran), and was rewarded within weeks of his death by the publication of his doctor's diary.'

Now Moran's book purports to be a diary but, as Gilbert discovered, it was a spurious diary. He records:

> **Perhaps the most disturbing discovery... came after I had finished the eighth and final volume of the biography, in which a major source... was the voluminous diary kept by Churchill's doctor, Lord Moran. Throughout the period of my researches the diary was closed to historians. Then, after the completion of the authorised life of the doctor, it was brought to a leading medical library in London. I asked for the diary entry for a single date (I wanted to reproduce [this] in facsimile in the second of my... document volumes [for the period]). To my dismay, not only for myself but for historical truth, I was told by the custodian of the papers that there was no entry for that day at all, even though an entry under that exact date appears in the published book. Even the entries that did exist, I was told, were 'not a diary in the accepted sense of the word.[34]**

That is to say, as a historian Moran was a fraudster. Worse still, events that were not dramatic enough already, he dramatised – something again that historians should avoid.

David Low, the New Zealand-born cartoonist, dramatised Churchill's career much more suitably, in a cartoon produced for his 80th birthday. It showed the protean range of activities (and uniforms) that Churchill had been involved in, during eight decades. The other art work associated with that birthday was Graham Sutherland's portrait, commissioned by Churchill's fellow parliamentarians. It was not a success. At the presentation its subject commented, 'It certainly combines force with candour'. Clemmie hated it, hid it away and ultimately had it destroyed. Certainly it did no more than document a tired, sick, ageing man, and quite failed to bring out the qualities that others could, even then, perceive of the central character of Low's cartoon. That central character, at the presentation ceremony, retained enough of what Sutherland missed, to deliver himself of the classic remark: 'It was the nation and the race dwelling all round the globe that

34 David Low's cartoon, celebrating Churchill's 80th birthday, portrayed the wide variety of activities, appointments, and uniforms that had given colour to his subject's career.

35 Sir Winston is greeted on arrival at Windsor for a Garter ceremony.

had the lion's heart. I had the luck to be called upon to give the roar.'

A more practical, and doubtless more popular, birthday gift was the Land Rover vehicle, registration number UKE80 – said to represent the UK and the Empire though, given Churchill's preoccupations at the time, 'Europe' would seem more apt – which was mildly adapted to make the passenger seat more welcoming, and in which he was able to be driven round the Chartwell fields. Remarkably, the Land Rover has survived in good condition, to be put up for auction in October 2012, when it fetched the sum of £129,000.

Table 8

THE EIGHTH DECADE 1944-54

Hernia repair

Strokes (2)

Transient Ischaemic Attacks [TIAs] (2)

Shoulder symptoms (assessed by Lord Brain)

Deafness (assessed by Sir Victor Negus)

Burns left hand

NOTES

1   It is popularly supposed that the 'iron curtain' metaphor came into being at Churchill's speech in Fulton, Missouri, in March 1946. This is not the case.

2   Hastings, M: *Finest years*. 2009; London: HarperCollins. p.449.

3   Gilbert, M: *In search of Churchill*. 1994; London: HarperCollins. In this book Gilbert (who first assisted Randolph Churchill, then took over the task of completing the Churchill biography and the companion volumes of documents) describes his quest for the recollections and judgments of those who knew and worked with Winston. He deals (pp. 196, 199, 209, 305) with Churchill's supposed heavy drinking – and also with the extent to which Moran was misled (pp. 209-210, pp. 211-2) by his ignorance of the connotation of the term 'black dog' when he laid emphasis on the extent of Churchill's depression. Moran, one feels, has a lot to answer for.

4   Townsend, P: *The last Emperor*. 1975; London: Weidenfeld & Nicolson. p. 202.

5   Nicolson, N: *Alex: the life of Field Marshal Earl Alexander of Tunis*. 1973; London: Weidenfeld & Nicolson. p.122.

6   Quoted in Soames, M: *Winston Churchill, his life as a painter*. London, 1990.

7   This material (as well as Harold Edwards' handwritten impressions from 1945) is in the Churchill Archives Centre. The 1945 notes – from which a brief extract has appeared in chapter IV of this book – make it plain how profound an impression Churchill could make on a perceptive witness.

8   This correspondence is in the Churchill Archives Centre [The Onslow collection, files 1-2]

9   Gilbert, M (2004): p. 1007-8.

10 One of Churchill's paintings of Marrakech from this visit recently changed hands at Sotheby's for £468,000, towards the upper end of the estimated price

range. It became the third most expensive of his works. He had given the painting to Harry Truman, the U S president, in the course of his Washington visit at the beginning of 1952; and Truman's daughter, Margaret Truman Daniels, put it up for sale just before her death in January 2008.

11   Dunhill's portrait by Sir James Gunn is in the collection of the Royal Australasian College of Surgeons, in Melbourne where he began his surgical career. The portrait is reproduced, and Dunhill's career briefly described, in my study of the *Portraits at the Royal Australasian College of Surgeons* [Melbourne, RACS: 1993. pp.78-80]

12   Moran, p.319.

13   Smith, JO (1967): *The Archibald Watson lecture; Stones, Diamonds, Coronets, Kings and their Surgical Custodians; Thomas Peel Dunhill*. Melbourne, McLaren & Co. pp.20, 34.

14   Jackson, BT (2005): Personal communication.

15   Moran, pp320-1.

16   Connolly, JE (2004) *J Am Coll Surg* 198: 175. See also Schein M & Rogers PN (2003) *J Am Coll Surg* 197: 313ff.

17   Brain, WR (2000): p.10.

18   Gilbert (2004) : p.1027.

19   Eastcott, HHG, Pickering, GW and Rob, CG. Reconstruction of internal carotid artery. *Lancet* 1954; II: 994. It is now possible to 'join the dots': Moran records that Churchill was seen by Charles Rob in 1959, at the time of the gangrenous fingertip, and again in 1960, these consultations relating to the problem of TIAs arising from emboli passing into his cerebral vessels. In *Churchill and America* [2006: London: Simon & Schuster, p.3 and n.] Martin Gilbert mentions Churchill having 'told one of his doctors' in 1960 about his descent, on his mother's side, from 'a Seneca Indian squaw'; and in a footnote he identifies this source as 'Recollections of Professor Rob, letter to the author, 17 November 1986.'

20 Brain: p.11.

21 Soames, M: *Clementine Churchill*. Revised edition, 2002: London: Doubleday. p. 558.

22 Gilbert [2004] p.1029.

23 Montague Browne, A: *Long Sunset*. 1995: London: Cassell. p. 143.

24 Gilbert [2004] p.1044.

25 *Ibid*. p.1052. Lady Lytton was the former Pamela Plowden, whom Churchill had courted in his India days. She once told Churchill's first Private Secretary, Eddie Marsh: 'The first time you meet Winston, you see all his faults, and the rest of your life you spend in discovering his virtues.' The Lyttons and the Churchills achieved a durable friendship.

26 This episode is examined by David Reynolds in *In Command of History* [London, Allen Lane: 2004]. Dorman-Smith, who had been Auchinleck's chief of staff, had retired to Eire, assumed an old family name to become Eric Dorman O'Gowan, and nursed his resentment over a decade. The dispute dragged on until 1954.

27 Gilbert [2004] p.1055.

28 In his introduction to his father's record of his *Encounters with Winston* Churchill, Michael Brain comments on the state of neurological diagnosis in the 1950s and 1960s, with its dependence on such matters as **the diminution or exaggeration of reflexes... It always seemed curious to me that, after a demonstration of changes in higher neurological function, an important determinant of the presence of an upper motor neurone lesion should depend on whether the big toe underwent plantar or dorsi flexion when the sole of the foot was scratched by a key! An up-going big toe, a positive plantar response, was indicative of an upper motor neurone (most often cerebral) lesion.**

The crude reflex response to such a stimulus is one of withdrawal – the great toe pulls up and *away from the key* – but modulation of the response by an intact pathway from the brain produces the down-going toe which would design to *push the key away*. In Churchill's case, Lord Brain was meticulous in recording these responses, which in each instance would yield useful confirmation of the impact of the stroke. His son's introduction goes on:

As a medical student on my father's "firm' at the London Hospital in 1952 I witnessed at his ward rounds the confirmatory plantar response being elicited by the key to his Rover.

No doubt the Rover key did duty for scratching the sole of Churchill's foot.

29 It is interesting to note that Churchill himself is recorded by Moran [p. 411] as enquiring, a mere three days after the 1953 stroke, 'Tell me, Charles, is there no operation for this kind of thing? I don't mind being a pioneer.' But the enquiry is documented, among other casual remarks, as if it were the sort of wild idea to which patients are attracted – and certainly not as something worthy of being followed up. It was this scepticism on the part of physicians that delayed the acceptance of Rob and Eastcott's initiative; and if we recall that they were surgeons at St Mary's, which was Moran's own hospital, we are left wondering …

30 Gilbert [2004] p.1061.

31 Churchill once described Dulles as 'the only bull that carries his china shop around with him'.

32 This episode may have illustrated the hazards of the cigar lit but not smoked; but such cigars as Churchill did smoke will have contributed to his vulnerability to strokes in his later years.

Rainsford Mowlem (1903-86) was put in charge of the North London centre at the outbreak of the 1939-45 war; this went to Hill End at St Albans and, after the war, to Mt Vernon Hospital at Northwood. The other three New Zealanders to become pioneers of British plastic surgery were Sir Harold Gillies, Sir Archibald McIndoe (who established the complementary, and better known, East Grinstead unit) and J N Barron. Sir Benjamin Rank's obituary of Mowlem was published in ANZ J Surg [1987; 57: 127]

33   *The Lancet's* criticism is recorded in: Davenport, G, McDonald, I & Moss-Gibbons, C (eds): *The Royal College of Physicians and its Collections.* 2001; London: James & James. p.152.

34   Gilbert, M [1994]: pp. 233, 238.

The phrase 'not a diary in the ordinary sense of the world' is firmly attached to the Moran documents. The catalogue to the collection in the Wellcome library stresses the use of the phrase as a disclaimer in Moran's prefaces, which conveniently overlooks the fact that, in the *Churchill – the struggle for survival* preface, it is applied not to the Churchill story but to the author's First War jottings. To a mere reader, a diary is either a diary or not.

By contrast with Moran's own sense of urgency in publishing, many of the documents in the collection were closed until 2026 or thereabouts; but in May 2010 I had the opportunity of examining one loose-leaf hardbound notebook which was out of quarantine.

Its contents are handwritten in blue ink in a tiny hand, and in many cases passages are underlined in red ink, or annotated in the margin, or rated as to 'publishability' according to a system which ranges from P? to P- and then on through P= to the insertion of four strokes for a 'must include' item.

The passages in this particular volume include the events of December 1941 in America, and are plainly a draft or rehearsal of what ultimately appeared in the book.

As the introduction to the catalogue observes, 'among the loose pages there seem to be few contemporary descriptions of events, though several may represent earlier drafts of thoughts which were later transcribed into the notebooks.'

On 1 January 2011 an accelerated release was announced in an adulatory statement by the Wellcome trust. It is not appropriate here to embark on a critique of this statement.

IX

LIBERTY ITSELF

I owe you what every
Englishman, woman and child does
– Liberty itself.

- Mary Soames (*née* Churchill) to WSC: 1964

Lord Moran, in his 'diary', records an occasion just a week after Churchill's eightieth birthday, when he visited his patient and

began to check the supply of pills, cachets and capsules on the table by his bed. Disprins and 'Lord Morans', majors and minors, reds and greens, babies and midgets, to drop into his own vocabulary.[1]

It was plainly a crowded table, crowded enough for Churchill to have rattled like a moneybox after taking his dose. The identity of some of these substances can be guessed at, and from a 'diary' entry thirteen years and 600 pages earlier, we know that 'reds' were barbiturate sleeping pills, of which Churchill was allowed two during the Washington visit that would be marked by his first coronary scare five days later. The administration of 'reds' is a recurring item in Moran's account thereafter (one every night, another if he woke during the night, as he would describe). Certainly the ill-effects of prolonged administration of barbiturates were less well understood half a century ago; but one has to wonder about their cumulative effect on Churchill.

The bedside table was not alone in providing for Churchill's needs. Early in 1955 Sir Alexander Cadogan called on him, and recorded that

on the floor by the side of the bed was a little metal pail with some water in it, destined presumably for the cigar ash and eventually for the stub. But as regards the ash at least, the PM did not seem to make much discrimination between the pail and the bed-clothes.[2]

* * *

Finally in March 1955 the prospect of a summit with the Russians was dashed by continued American timidity, and in April Churchill announced his intention to retire as Prime Minister. Earlier that day, visiting the House of Commons for the first time, I had listened to what was destined to be his final prime ministerial speech. He used his deafness as a weapon; if he had a response to an interjection, it came out like a rifle shot; if the interjection caught him unprepared he would turn to Eden, ask loudly, 'What did he say? What? What?' By the time Eden had repeated the remark three or four times it sounded absurd; but by then the Old

Man had his response ready to bark it out and go on with his speech. On the night before his trip to Buckingham Palace to tender his resignation, he and his wife had The Queen and Prince Philip as dinner guests at No 10.

Immediately after Easter he and Clementine, with 'Prof' (by now Lord Cherwell) and the faithful Jock Colville (not yet Sir John), went to Sicily for a fortnight's rest, staying at a hotel in Syracuse. He wrote to The Queen, acknowledging her farewell letter on his retirement (handed to him as he boarded the aircraft) and described to her how the place 'rises out of the sinister quarries in which six thousand Athenian prisoners of war were toiled and starved to death in 413 BC'. At the age of 80, he retained his ability to identify the historical perspective of his travels – but this vacation also provided evidence of his persisting strengths as a forward thinker.

* * *

Clementine was, at this time, plagued by the pain of her neuritis, and unable to take any very active part in things. And it rained! The three men therefore found themselves much driven to the process of 'chewing the rag'. 'Prof' had been concerned for some while that Britain was in danger of losing her position in the world of scientific and technological innovation. She had entered the wartime alliance with the two priceless initiatives of radar and penicillin, which were freely shared with, and thereafter exploited by, her American ally. She had been foremost in nuclear research, and here too she had been subsumed into the 'Allied' – in effect, the American – programme, and thereafter patronised in matters atomic. Churchill had been disturbed by his inability to do much during his second term as Prime Minister to rectify the position.

The inspiration was Jock Colville's: let funds contributed at the time of Churchill's 80th birthday serve as pump-priming capital, he proposed; and let an 'institution' be formed, dedicated to correcting the deficiencies identified by Lord Cherwell and thus capable of serving not only as a living memorial of Churchill himself, but incidentally as a retirement interest for him. Though not a scientist by upbringing and education, Churchill had many of the instincts of a scientist and had a worthy background as a promoter of scientific initiatives in time of war. He also had the ability, shared with 'Prof', to make scientific information comprehensible: an ability which stood him in good stead during the Locust Years, when he depended on his journalism for his living – or at least for the more gracious parts of it.

I have read a number of his journalistic essays: one in particular, is entitled *The mystery of the body*. It was written in 1939 for the *News of the World* – yes: he even wrote for that lately-defunct publication. Not used at the time, it was published in 1942 by the *Sunday Despatch*. It would not disgrace a medical undergraduate who is studying human biology and has been set the challenge of describing the human body, its anatomy and physiology, in sixteen pages.

The story of what (after a false cast or two) became Churchill College is peripheral enough to a study of Churchill's medical history that only a few points need be noted here. The first is that the trust which raised funds under Churchill's own chairmanship was at the same time distinguished and widely representative; the second, that it was a generous flow of opinion which enabled the foundation of the new College at Cambridge, given that Lindemann's great challenge, when he was appointed to his Oxford chair in 1919, had been to reverse the influence of his predecessor Robert Bellamy Clifton and make his Clarendon laboratory a credible rival for Cambridge's Cavendish.[3]

But, in a story peppered with ironies, it is one of the happiest that (although Churchill College was founded to promote quality education in science and technology, and has achieved richly in this field) the jewel in its crown has proved to be what might be considered its 'arts faculty'. The Churchill Archives Centre - situated within the College and well integrated into its activities – has achieved an enviable reputation as 'a major centre of historical research into what might be called the Churchill Era, where scholars will be able to find a great mass of inter-related material gathered together under a single roof': for that is what Sir John Cockcroft, the College's first Master, wrote in July 1967, in a letter setting out his own aspirations when an archives centre was first contemplated.

It is pleasant to be able to record that Churchill's own health was well enough preserved to allow him to take part in a symbolic tree-planting ceremony on 17 October 1959, on the site of his future eponymous College. He survived until after the opening in June 1964, though by then he was too frail to attend; and in his lifetime he became the College's first Honorary Fellow.

36a,b At the founding of Churchill College, on 17 October 1959, Sir Winston planted an oak tree (left). It has grown into a massive specimen, in front of which stands the director of the *Churchill Archive Centre*, Mr Allen Packwood (right).

* * *

Eighteen months after the Sicily visit he had another stroke while holidaying in the South of France; then, just two days after he was fit enough to return to Britain the Suez debacle erupted, and the United States sabotaged what was in any case an unfortunate attempt by Britain and France to coerce Egypt by military means – unfortunate because, as Bernard Fergusson described in his history of Combined Operations, an exemplary military operation was carried out in spite of constant political interference.

> **They had every right to say 'Go' and 'Stop', to flash Green or Red; but no commander should be asked to conduct an operation in flickering conditions of amber.**[4]

To such a level had Britain's status and performance subsided, in the space of less than two years since Churchill's retirement.

Sir Russell Brain saw Churchill again on his return to London; his notes record that his patient had been seen at the time of the stroke by Dr John Roberts, the family physician in Monaco, who recorded loss of speech and weakness of the right arm and leg. Brain found it difficult to detect a carotid pulse on either side of the neck.

Eighteen months later, at Beaverbrook's villa at Cap d'Ail, Churchill suffered yet another bout of pneumonia. When he recovered, his friend Brendan Bracken wrote to him:

I am pleased and relieved beyond all telling by your rapid recovery. If you were to write a book on "Health without Rules" it would outsell all your other books.[5]

But it is interesting to notice how often these various medical adventures seem to have overtaken Churchill when he was supposedly on holiday round the Mediterranean. It may be, of course, that he had more opportunity of inhaling cigar smoke under these conditions, as opposed to flourishing a cigar while making a V-sign for the benefit of onlookers.

But then, and in spite of Bracken's cheerful tribute, the pneumonia on that 1958 occasion was followed by the curious business of the jaundice.

37 These views of Sir Winston Churchill, attending a fund-raising gala in his Woodford electorate in June 1958, show the scar of his 1931 vehicle accident in New York. They also show the play of his emotions: expressing his opinion of the afternoon heat (left), examining the audience (centre), and recognising an old friend (right).

* * *

At the onset of the pneumonia Moran had been called out to France, had prescribed a fresh antibiotic and, on 7 March according to his diary, returned to England.

On 24 March he was 'staying with the Freybergs in

the Norman Tower at Windsor' (after his term as governor-general of New Zealand, Lord Freyberg became Deputy Constable and Lieutenant-Governor of Windsor Castle)[6] where a telephone call from France informed him that, since Moran's return to England, his patient 'had had two bouts of fever'. He flew to Nice the next day, where

> **it had been noticed that Winston was yellow, but this was thought to be due to the antibiotic I had prescribed. In fact he is suffering from obstructive jaundice, caused either by a stone or by an infection of the bile passages.'[7]**

We are not told the evidence on which this splendid *ex cathedra* diagnosis was based, which is unusual, given that Moran commonly describes the investigations he ordered and Churchill's reaction – hostile, suspicious or enthusiastic according to the situation – to them. Nor do we learn which of the possible causes of Churchill's obstructive jaundice proved to have been responsible, or indeed what if any treatment was followed. One thing we can note is that, ten days after Churchill's repatriation to England at the beginning of April, there was another episode of atrial fibrillation; but we are left wondering: was the confidence of the Moranian diagnosis augmented by hindsight?

* * *

There was another small stroke in April 1959,[8] but Churchill insisted on visiting America once more, staying at the White House with Eisenhower – his friend Ike. He may have been infuriated, often, by American naiveté or intransigence, but his friendship with Ike was deep and sincere.

On his return he went cruising in the Onassis yacht *Christina*, then came back to La Pausa at Roquebrune before returning to another election campaign. After the election, it was to Monte Carlo that he and Clementine went in search of sun, before he rejoined *Christina* for a West Indies cruise. To his daughter Diana, on his return, he remarked 'My life is over, but it is not yet ended.' A schedule that would have been bruising for a younger man made the remark seem disingenuous. And yet, by now, his deafness had become no longer a weapon but a barrier, which drove him into a state of reverie that became more and more difficult for his family and friends to penetrate.

In November 1960 he had a further small stroke, enough to put him in bed under the care of two Antipodean nurses, whose notes have been preserved,[9] but not enough to prevent him from celebrating his 86th birthday at lunch with his family. These notes create the image of an old man, frustrated beyond endurance by his frailties, and being cosseted by a stream of consultant visitors at the instance of Lord Moran. The neck and shoulder pain that had troubled him so much in recent years was again in evidence, and he was seen by Professor H J (later Sir Herbert) Seddon and his senior registrar, Mr Philip Yeoman. On occasions it all became too much: on 4 December 1960 the record breaks out: 'Extremely difficult and abusive!... very uncooperative. Calmed down after about one hour; ate normal breakfast. Rather subdued for rest of morning.'

Not long afterwards he fell in his bedroom and sustained a crush fracture of one of his thoracic vertebrae; it seems likely that this fall also stirred up the degenerative changes in his cervical spine, because Sir Russell Brain was called to see him on account of painful numbness of the left index finger, and attributed this to pressure on the 6th cervical nerve root.[10]

Two Monte Carlo visits later, in June 1962, he fell and broke his left hip. He told his Secretary, 'I want to die in England,' and the wish was enough to prompt Harold Macmillan, now Prime Minister, to send an RAF Comet to bring him home – but not yet home to die.[11]

Herbert Seddon, who had seen him after his stroke a couple of years earlier, was called to advise, and his senior registrar Philip Yeoman, joined the team.[12] Churchill was treated in the Middlesex Hospital under the care of Philip Newman, an orthopaedic surgeon whose background must certainly have commended him to his patient, for Newman was one of those who, graduating in 1934 and obtaining the FRCS in 1938, came to personal and professional maturity during the War, at the end of which he was a lieutenant-colonel with a DSO and an MC, and an enviable reputation for daring escape and distinguished service.

The fracture was far enough down the neck of the femur not to jeopardise the blood supply of the spherical femoral head, and Newman was able to align the fragments and hold them with a trifin nail driven up the centre of the neck of the femur, joined to a metal plate affixed to the shaft of the bone. The result was immaculate.

From correspondence in the Churchill Archive, it is possible to identify the actors in this drama: the anaesthetists were Drs O P Dinnick and D H P Cope,

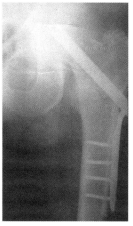

38a,b Churchill's hip fracture was treated by Philip Newman, the fragments aligned and fixed with a trifin nail and plate

both of them on the Middlesex staff and both Fellows, from 1953, of the Faculty of Anaesthetists (which had been formed within the Royal College of Surgeons in 1948, and would become a College in its own right fifty years later).

The members of the team were given framed photographs of their eminent patient: the largest one went to Philip Newman; Philip Yeoman and five others received photographs one size smaller. Yeoman's recognition included volumes of the *English Speaking Peoples* series; acknowledging his gifts, he wrote that he was 'proud to be asked to join the surgical team during your last illness'[13] (and one has to wonder if he, a product of University College Hospital, reckoned a foray to the Middlesex as a proud moment in itself). Philip Newman himself was given a silver salver; his 'English Speaking Peoples' moment would come in 1976, as host to the Combined Orthopaedic meeting.

An obituary in the journal *British Orthopaedic News* records an intriguing aspect of this surgical exercise. Of the orthopaedic surgeon Henry Piggott [1925-2009] it notes that

Henry was senior registrar to Philip Newman when Sir Winston Churchill fractured his hip. As if suturing the wound was not responsibility enough, Harry was entrusted with the duty of allocating visiting priority between former Presidents of the United States, Fields [*sic*] Marshal, other senior military figures, diplomats, politicians and others![14]

A nurse who was working in the Woolavington Wing ('a private wing that mostly catered for the aristocracy', she describes it) recalls an old man, somewhat confused after his numerous strokes, whose room smelt of smoke (though she never saw him smoking), who had some evidently alcoholic drink in a large tumbler alongside his bed, from which he would 'just sip away' – and who 'appeared to be on a lot of medication'.

Two letters written to the Young Conservatives in his electorate show, in their respective signatures, his ability to bounce back from disability. In the first, in September 1962, three months after his hip fracture, the writing is as shaky as one might expect from an aged and ailing man; but by May 1963 his signature had regained its pristine quality.

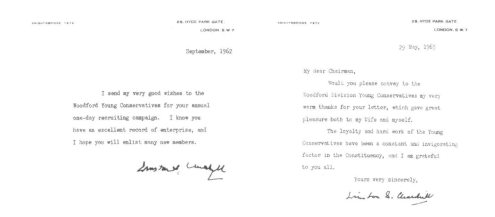

39 Comparison of the signatures on these two letters to the Young Conservatives of Woodford (one in September 1962, the other May 1963) shows Churchill's recuperative abilities, even in his high eighties.

Churchill was, however, to experience another stroke in July 1963, followed in October by the shock of his daughter Diana's suicide. His last visit to the Commons, in a wheelchair, was in July 1964; his last public appearance a V-sign to the crowd outside his house, on his 90th birthday.

In January 1965 he had a final and massive stroke; even then he lingered for two weeks. His death on 24 January had the added significance that this was the anniversary of his father's death. Hundreds of thousands filed past at his lying-in-state in Westminster Hall. His funeral brought London nearer to a standstill than the Blitz could ever do. As his coffin was borne by launch on his final journey along the Thames the dockland cranes dipped in salute. His had been a full life: full of achievement, full of controversy, full of excitement - and full also of medical adventure.

40 As the launch *Havengore*, carrying Churchill's coffin, made its way to Waterloo pier, the dockland cranes lowered their jibs in salute.

* * *

Since Churchill's death, there has been a further accretion of myth, much of it concerning his medical conditions and his lifestyle. Certainly his tastes, for good food, good wine and good cigars cannot be doubted, and are, in any case, consistent with his aristocratic heritage and the social *mores* of his youth. Alanbrooke records one quiet lunch he and his chief shared during their common convalescence (Churchill from pneumonia, Brooke from a severe dose of influenza) in March 1943:

> **Plover's eggs, chicken broth, chicken pie, chocolate soufflé and, with it a bottle of champagne, followed by port and brandy.**

Who would not regard such a menu as conducive to convalescence? And we know that it would have been a good champagne: Churchill's taste in later life ran to Pol Roger.

As for cigars, they were not ideal therapy for a man prone to pneumonia, but that respiratory weakness was evident in his childhood, and far antedated the liking he gained in Cuba at the time of his 21st birthday. It may be conjectured that many (perhaps most) smouldered alongside him more than they were smoked – indeed, the most dramatic ill-effect of his smoking habits occurred at the Trinity House luncheon, that day in 1953.

I have considered earlier the matter of depression; this I regard as a largely Moran-inspired myth, which can be traced to Moran's ignorance of nanny-speak (and indeed of Samuel Johnson).

I suppose it is a back-handed tribute to Churchill that he attracted such a flowering of legend. Unfortunately, as I have come to appreciate while describing my recent study activities to friends and acquaintances, the common perception of Churchill is built, quite substantially, on myths which do not stand up well to investigation.

It is to be hoped that this short study of a great man will lead to a better appreciation of his greatness, a more sympathetic understanding of those genuine weaknesses that drove Alanbrooke sometimes close to distraction, coupled with a rejection of the cruder myths (whether political or socio-medical), and an awareness of just how much illness and injury he surmounted.

For in both medical and political terms he was indeed a survivor. And Alanbrooke (though well aware of his master's weaknesses) could write of him:

He is quite the most wonderful man I have ever met, and it is a source of never-ending interest studying him and getting to realise that occasionally such human beings make their appearance on earth – human beings who stand head and shoulders above all others.[15]

Table 9

THE FINAL DECADE 1954-65

Strokes (5)

Pneumonia

Jaundice, obstructive ?cause

Atrial fibrillation

Gangrene fingertip, embolic

Fracture hip

Died 24 January 1965 after final massive stroke

NOTES

1   Moran, p. 619 (and cf. p. 11, p. 236, p.288)

2   Dilks, D (1971): *op. cit.*

3   Clifton occupied the Oxford Chair 'of Experimental Philosophy' (or, as
    we might say: Physics) 1865-1915. He eschewed research, believing that it
    'betrayed a certain restlessness of mind'.

4   Fergusson, B.E: *The watery Maze.* 1961; London: Collins. p.403.

5   Gilbert, M [2004] p.1098.

6   Bernard Cyril Freyberg, 1st Baron Freyberg of Wellington, New Zealand and
    Munstead, Surrey [1889-1963], was brought to Wellington by his parents
    as a two-year old. He and his four brothers attended the local Wellington
    College; he trained as a dentist, but found his vocation at the outbreak of the
    First War when, arriving with a letter of introduction to Churchill, he was
    commissioned into the Royal Naval Division (one of Churchill's initiatives as
    First Lord). A champion swimmer, he won his first DSO for swimming along
    the shore to plant decoy flares the night before the Gallipoli landings. His VC
    came for sustained gallantry at Beaucourt the following year.
        Between the wars he and Churchill became good friends (and Paul
    Freyberg's biography of his father describes one dinner party that his parents
    hosted, at which the men talked long into the night. When they went in
    search of their wives only Barbara Freyberg was still on the scene. It cost
    Bernard several boxes of expiatory chocolates).
        In the Second War Freyberg commanded 2 NZ Division throughout the
    Mediterranean campaigns, and in 1946 he became governor-general of the
    country to which he had given such service. His term was extended to six
    years and he was raised to the peerage at the end of it.
        Churchill was, I think, fascinated by Freyberg as a man of courage.
    Moran [p. 575] records one instance of Churchill, in reminiscent mood,
    describing 'how he had asked Bernard Freyberg the number of his wounds,

how he answered 'thirty-three', and had stripped
and shown Winston the scars.'

But it was not simply Freyberg's courage that
Churchill admired. In 1940, when the New Zealand
Division was scattered between Arundel and the
Middle East, and Freyberg 'commuting' between
the two portions of his command, Churchill had
the general write an appreciation of the Middle
East situation. It was a most perceptive document,
and Reynolds [*In command of history*, London:
Allen Lane, 2004] sees it as a factor in Freyberg's
appointment, the next year, to command the
defence of Crete.

That appointment was what is nowadays
called 'a hospital pass'; for no campaign has been
so influenced by air superiority (on the part of the
Germans) and insufficiency of resources (on the
part of the defenders).

41 The friendship between
Churchill and Freyberg
dated from 1914; and it
can reasonably be claimed
that there was an element
of hero-worship on
Churchill's part. Here they
are deep in discussion on
one of the PM's visits to
the New Zealand Division
in North Africa.

7   Moran, pp. 732-6.

8   In *Encounters with Winston Churchill*, the Brains appear to have blended the
     record of two strokes, in April and October 1959: the entry dated 15 October
     relates, I believe, to the events of 15 April; but convincingly it identifies
     embolus formation as responsible for both the stroke and the dry gangrene of
     the little finger.

9   A reporter's note book bears the name of the New Zealand nurse, Margaret
     Taylor, and includes nursing notes in various hands covering the period
     November- December 1960. Filed with the book [WCHL 6/66 in the
     Churchill Archives Centre] is a reference for the Australian nurse, Muriel
     Thomson, signed by Winston and countersigned by Clementine, which
     testifies to her being 'reliable, efficient, trustworthy and forthright in all
     her dealings with myself and other members of my family and my staff'.
     It credits her with 'tact, diplomacy and discretion' over a period involving
     '6 visits to Monte Carlo, and to the West Indies in "Christina", Mr Aristottle
     Onassi's [*sic*] yacht.'

10   Or the 7th cervical nerve root: the precise distribution varies.

11   In the book *In search of Churchill* [p.271], Martin Gilbert tells
     ... a story (almost certainly embellished)... which had been sent to me
     by a correspondent, of Churchill resisting the efforts of French doctors
     to operate on him after his fall in the South of France towards the end
     of his life, when he began to mutter at them, "You bloody butchers!
     I won't allow you to cut me up. If you try, I will drag you through the
     law courts," which a friend who was with him quickly translated: 'Mr
     Churchill thanks you for your consideration, but has decided that he
     will fly home for the operation.'

12   Montague Browne, in his reminiscences *Long Sunset*, (p. 313) writes that
     Philip Yeoman was chosen by Seddon to carry out the operation. I think he
     has telescoped his Philips.

13 Correspondence relating to this episode is in the Churchill Archives Centre: the list of recipients of photographs at CHUR 1/62/119, Philip Yeoman's letter CHUR 1/62/88.

14 Obituary, *British Orthopaedic News*. 2010; 43: 46.

15 Bryant, p.8.

X

GLOW-WORM

We are all worms.
But I do believe that
I am a glow-worm.

- WSC to Violet Asquith, 1906[1]

The awareness of genius is an uncomfortable thing – much more uncomfortable than the delusion of genius which more commonly afflicts politicians. I think Churchill's earliest years – years of aristocratic loneliness, of the toy soldiers which were one of his father's kinder gifts (and which fascinated the child, besides bringing out his latent strategic talent), of his teachers' failure to engage his imagination or intellect – all these things, I believe, combined to make him the person he became. For it is my view that out of his juvenile miseries and musings came the resolution that he would prove himself to himself, and thereby to the world. This in turn created the sense of destiny that would save the world in 1940.

To be sure it was written in retrospect, but the final paragraph of *The Gathering Storm* (the first volume of his account of the Second War), describing his feelings on the night of 10 May 1940, a few hours after he had become Prime Minister, conveys this sense very precisely:

> **I cannot conceal from the reader of this truthful account that as I went to bed about 3 a.m., I was conscious of a profound sense of relief. At last I had the authority to give directions over the whole scene. I felt as if I were walking with destiny, and that my past life had been but a preparation for this hour and this trial… I thought I knew a good deal about it all, and I was sure I should not fail. Therefore, although impatient for the morning, I slept soundly, and had no need for cheering dreams. Facts are better than dreams.**

* * *

Whether from a sense of invincibility or for the sheer excitement of it, he was always one to take risks. Indeed, in the days when he supported himself by his journalism, he contributed an article on this aspect of his behaviour.[2]

In it he quoted the Australian poet Adam Lindsay Gordon [1833-70]:

> **No game was ever yet worth a rap**
> **For a rational man to play,**
> **Into which no accident, no mishap**
> **Could possibly find its way.**

He went on to describe in some detail two episodes from his youth: first, the 1893 game in which he attempted to escape his pursuers by leaping off the bridge across to the young tree: 'The argument,' he wrote, 'was correct; the data were absolutely wrong.' He was unconscious for three days, and it was two or three months before he could leave his bed.

His second episode came just before he started at Sandhurst, when he and his brother Jack were on a walking tour round the lake of Lausanne. Winston and another boy were out in a rowing boat; it was a calm day and they stripped off for a swim. But their boat had, as he recalled all too vividly, a red awning, and it began to drift as a breeze got up They swam after it, almost reached it – and then came another puff of wind, and another. It was not long before the other boy was in trouble. Winston was a good swimmer, having represented his house at Harrow. It fell to him to overtake the boat. 'I now saw Death as near as I believe I have ever seen him,' he wrote of the pursuit. But he caught up.

* * *

42 After the liberation of Paris in 1944 the British Ambassador hosted a luncheon at which Churchill met Jacques and Odette Pol-Roger; out of this meeting grew an enduring friendship, such that Churchill named one of his racehorses Pol Roger, while the champagne dynasty continues to name some of its outstanding vintages after him. Such an arrangement would, in modern parlance, be described as a 'win-win situation'.

Churchill's background gives a clue to the realities of one of the favourite Churchill myths – the one that has him an alcoholic. He was, as we have seen, close to the heart of the aristocracy, and grew up in an atmosphere of 'gracious living'. This developed in him the attitude of a *bon viveur*.[3] His choice of drinks was somewhat limited: champagne (good champagne: in later life his own choice was Pol Roger); whisky, brandy. He tolerated 'lesser' white wines, he had little liking for reds; when his son-in-law, Christopher Soames, smuggled in a bottle of claret, the Old Man would notice and – with suitable rhetoric – would grumble.

He could derive some amusement from his assault on the wine mountain of Epernay. In Sir Ian Jacob's biography is recorded an episode on the train journey to take ship and meet President Roosevelt off Newfoundland in August 1941:

> Just as lunch was finishing the PM suddenly jumped up in his place, put his head over the back of his seat and said, 'Prof, what is 24 times 365?' Out came the Prof's slide rule, and after considerable delay the answer was given as nearly 9000. 'Well,' said the Prime Minister, '9000 bottles of champagne are not too bad. I can look back on a well-spent life. Prof, what size swimming bath would that amount of champagne full?' More slide-rule, 'Well, it would easily get inside this compartment.' 'Ho,' said the Prime Minister, 'I do not think much of that. I shall have to improve on that in the future.'[4]

After Churchill's stroke in 1953, Moran recorded,

> He took refuge in levity: 'I am trying, Charles, to cut down alcohol. I have knocked off brandy' – the coming sally made him smile - 'and take cointreau instead. I disliked whisky at first. It was only when I was a subaltern in India, and there was a choice between drinking dirty water and dirty water with some whisky in it, that I got to like it I have always, since that time, made a point of keeping in practice.

and then, disapprovingly, Moran goes on:

> But since the stroke he has discovered that alcohol does him no good. It makes his speech more difficult to understand and fuddles what is left of his wits.[5]

But his close colleagues have testified to the powers of serial dilution which allowed him to keep a 'full' glass of spirits by his side for long periods.

And, although it was designed to point a simile, there was his own observation on the merits of champagne:

A single glass of champagne imparts a feeling of exhilaration. The nerves are braced; the imagination is agreeably stirred; the wits become more nimble. A bottle produces a contrary effect. Excess causes a comatose insensibility. So it is with war: and the quality of both is best discovered by sipping.

Commenting on the additional duty on sparkling wines imposed in Britain (back in the 1860s) an Australian vigneron noted that, as a result,

the drinking of what is essentially a healthful tonic for the stomach has become an affair for wealthy ostentation.[6]

For Churchill, I believe, it was the 'healthful tonic' qualities in champagne that mattered.

'I should make it clear,' wrote his last Private Secretary, Anthony Montague Browne, 'that although WSC enjoyed his drink, during the twelve and a half years I spent with him, I never saw him the worse for wear, although he once said he was.'[7] Indeed it was possible for someone very close to him to stress the point to me that 'of course, he smoked too much; he drank too much (we all did in those days) – but I have *never ever* seen him drunk.' Churchill himself, typically, saw it in historical perspective:

One of the few survivals from the age of rotten boroughs is the rotten insinuation that men in the public eye are alcoholics unless they are teetotallers.[8]

And, as my friend Donald Simpson pointed out, 'Alcoholics rarely live to 90, or make fine speeches at nearly 80.'

* * *

The next taunt that has followed Churchill through much of his career is that his judgment was unsound, and that he undertook various madcap schemes against the wishes of his elders and betters. A couple of First War episodes illustrate the process of approval-become-derision that beset him.

On 22 September 1914 three large armoured cruisers, *Aboukir*, *Hogue* and *Cressy*, were patrolling a beat in the North Sea; so was the German submarine U-9. Gilbert writes:

> **The Germans sank [the] three British cruisers, with the loss of 1,459 officers and men. The three ships were on patrol that day off the Dogger Bank, despite Churchill's written instruction four days earlier that they 'ought not to continue on this beat' because of the risks. His instruction was unknown to the public, and subsequently kept secret by the Government. As a result, he was blamed for the loss of the ships and their men.[9]**

And that, we need to recall, was a mere six weeks after the First Lord had gained plaudits for having the fleet in a state of readiness at the outbreak of war.

Ten days later things were becoming desperate in Belgium, and Churchill was called back from setting out on a visit to France (his fifth, already), this one to review the arrangements between Sir John French (the commander-in-chief of the British Expeditionary Force) and sundry Royal Marine elements – airmen and armoured car operators – who were providing a force to harry the German lines of communication.

The summons to return was occasioned by the news that the Belgian government was about to abandon Antwerp, the fortress-port which stood on the Germans' route to the Channel ports of Dunkirk and Calais. Kitchener the War minister wished to send a British relief force to the city, but the situation was obscure and the danger immediate. Churchill, who had planned to spend the night in Dunkirk, offered to go on to Antwerp and there obtain better information and seek to stiffen Belgian resolve. His offer was received with enthusiasm.

That night, 2 October, a special train took him to Dover, a destroyer to Ostend; he then drove to Antwerp. From the Belgian prime minister he obtained agreement to try to hold out for ten days, provided British reinforcements could be sent. From his own para-naval resources Churchill was able to offer a Marine brigade from

Dunkirk overnight, with the Royal Naval Division to follow. All this was endorsed by Kitchener, and by Asquith the prime minister.

But then Churchill, in his eagerness, offered to take over command provided he could be given appropriate rank and authority (he had, after all, more experience of soldiering than many commanders of the period) 'because,' he reported, 'I am sure this will afford the best prospect of a victorious result to an enterprise in which I am deeply involved.' Kitchener would have given him rank as lieutenant-general; but those back in London who were disposed to snigger – notably Asquith himself [10] – seized their opportunity.

By midday on 6 October, 8,000 British troops were in the city, and Churchill's more 'orthodox' replacement, General Rawlinson, arrived later with a force of 40,000 more following him. By then, unfortunately, the Belgians had lost heart and, on 8 October, with the city in flames, the British withdrawal began. Antwerp surrendered on 10 October; but in the week that had been gained the main British army had been able to return to the Channel coast and to re-form in Flanders.

That was not achievement enough, of course, for Churchill's enemies, and especially the Conservatives, from whom he had resigned ten years before; and another black mark was chalked up against the man who would shortly be saddled, equally unjustly, with the blame for Gallipoli.

The hurt that Gallipoli caused him can be judged by a passage in his review, in 1932, of a book by his 'foul-weather friend' Max Aitken, Lord Beaverbrook:

> **Broken irretrievably by my failure to compel the prosecution of the naval attack on the Dardanelles, saddled with the odium of the military mismanagement which I had no power to prevent, I dwelt in a chill and forbidding twilight until... July 1917 [when he was made minister of munitions].**

* * *

Churchill was, as we can see in these small cameos, a man often subjected to criticism and (surprisingly, perhaps, in view of what many saw as a cocksure attitude) able to be wounded by it. The evidence of those who knew him best seems to have been that – although he could be infuriating – he was a lovable man. His marriage to Clementine was a rich and lasting partnership between two strong people, and their love shines through their correspondence for all to see.

At one end of Churchill's career, Clementine's mother, Blanche Hozier, wrote concerning her prospective son-in-law to an old friend, the poet Wilfrid Scawen Blunt, at the time of her daughter's engagement: 'He is gentle and affectionate to those he loves, much hated by those who have not come under his personal charm.'[11]

And towards the other end Harold Edwards, who treated Churchill's hernia in 1945, noted in his diary:

His face, when he is pleased with a thought of his, or a situation conjured up by a remark of someone else, wrinkles up like a babe's – like Puck's.

* * *

43a In his youth his collars threatened to trim his earlobes.

b ...a spotted bow tie, to complete an ensemble of black jacket and waistcoat, striped trousers and ample watchchain.

He could be vain, of course, and his vanity found expression in his dress code. But what began as a harmless eccentricity became a vital part of the *persona* that stirred a nation. In his young days his wing collars threatened to trim his earlobes; he soon settled into the routine display of a spotted bow tie, completing an outfit of black coat and waistcoat (the coat itself varied from time to time and occasion to occasion, but was commonly either behind or ahead of current fashion), striped trousers and of course an ample watch chain. And his hats were a cartoonist's delight.

His wedding outfit attracted the derision of the *Tailor and Cutter* magazine: '"Neither fish, flesh nor fowl!"... one of the greatest failures as a wedding garment we have ever seen, giving the wearer a sort of glorified coachman appearance.' And certainly the photograph which shows him arriving with his best man, Lord Hugh

Cecil, shows him looking as if both top hat and frock coat might with advantage have been one size larger.

44 The magazine *Tailor and Cutter* was highly critical of Churchill's wedding outfit.

But uniforms fascinated him. His wide range of connexions and appointments entitled him to wear numerous military or near-military garments during his wartime escapades, and a number of these are on display in the 'Uniform Room' at Chartwell. His favourite seems to have been that of his appointment in 1939 as Honorary Air Commodore of 615 (County of Surrey) Squadron of the Royal Auxiliary Air Force, which acquired pilot's wings in 1943; but he also made widespread use of his service dress as honorary colonel of the 4th Hussars. Curiously, this jacket bore the buttons of the Royal Sussex Regiment, as did the tropical service dress he wore in Cairo in 1942. At sea, he had the undress uniform of an Elder Brother of Trinity House.

45a,b Churchill's dress sense managed to embrace the splendour of his full dress uniform as Lord Warden of the Cinque Ports, or the informality of the siren suit which could be put on in a few seconds In this detail from a group photograph of 1941, he stands alongside his loyal Private Secreary Jock (later Sir John) Colville, who was leaving to serve in the RAF.

Then there were the ceremonial uniforms: the full dress of a Privy Councillor was widely used on formal occasions when he was appointed to the Council in 1907; he became entitled to the full dress uniform of an Elder Brother of Trinity House in 1913 while he was First Lord of the Admiralty; and in 1941 he became Lord Warden of the Cinque Ports (only the second commoner, after the Duke of Wellington, to hold the office). This latter he wore under his Garter robes for the Coronation in 1953. As for the Trinity House full dress, Paul Johnson recalls the occasion when General de Gaulle 'asked him what it was, and received the mystifying reply, "Je suis un frère aîné de la Sainte Trinité."'[12]

Paradoxically, he was as celebrated for devising 'the siren suit' as for his more orthodox and formal items of dress. This derived from the boiler suits he wore when bricklaying at Chartwell during the 1930s and, with a long zip down the front, enabled him to be up and dressed at great speed during air raids and the like. He grew to like the concept so much that he applied it to rich velvet fabrics for evening wear at home (there is a splendid burgundy example in the Churchill Museum under Whitehall.)

What might earlier have been dismissed as a harmless eccentricity came into its own in 1940, when all these items of dress (and the hats, at some times more suitable than others) served their purpose in identifying a leader who could inspire a nation: something which had been quite beyond his predecessors in office.

Then there was the V-sign. Unlike 1914, when an outbreak of pious xenophobia drove the First Sea Lord from office and German composers were deemed unworthy to be heard,[13] one of the early means of offering encouragement to the population of occupied Europe after mid-1940 was the playing of Beethoven's 5th Symphony, with its opening notes sounding out the Morse sign for 'V'. And it took no time at all for a patriot in Occupied Europe to scrape a 'V' on a wall and move on, encouraged by the gesture.

46 Winston gives his celebrated 'V sign', to the delight of the men aboard *Queen Mary* who had just accompanied him to the US in May 1943.

Churchill's counterpoint to this was his adoption of the hand gesture that became his trademark: and this happens to provide a fragment of indirect evidence concerning his use of alcohol. In giving the V-sign Churchill would hold his ring and little fingers bent into the palm, to throw the index and middle fingers into prominence. This position (ring and little fingers bent) is commonly forced upon those who suffer from Dupuytren's contracture, a thickening of the tissues under the skin of the palm, which then shorten and drag the fingers down.[14] Now Dupuytren's disease is commoner in alcoholics than in the community at large; and a casual observer studying a photograph of Churchill's V-sign hand might wonder if there were a medical necessity for the two bent digits.

I have examined the bronze cast of Churchill's hand made by Oscar Nemon, now in the Churchill Archives Centre: the palm skin shows no thickening and the fingers no restriction of their ability to straighten. Neither do those photographs in which he is not making the V sign. A diagnosis of Dupuytren's disease affecting the ring and little fingers (and any implications that might be drawn from it) is not tenable. Indeed Anthony Montague Browne, who was Churchill's last Private Secretary, and served him loyally for a dozen years, remarked that 'there was something aesthetically appealing about those hands' – and, reflecting on their appearance even in death, he chose the word 'beautiful'.[15]

* * *

And what are we to make, after all this, of Charles McMoran Wilson? The continued prevalence of his nickname – 'Corkscrew Charlie' – that I encountered when visiting the United Kingdom in 2005 and subsequently, has to tell us a lot about the man. But there is more substance than that to a front-line medical officer who is awarded a Military Cross, which was Wilson's achievement in 1916, after two years spent in the trenches. There he observed the men he cared for, likening their response to the dangers about them to the management of a bank account, and observing how, at the point where the account dipped 'into the red' fear took over. Out of these observations came a small book, which he published in 1945 (he describes its birth pangs in his book about Churchill). He had settled on the title *The anatomy of fear*; at Churchill's suggestion he changed this to *The anatomy of courage* and the book achieved high regard (though Moran chose not to broadcast the source of that inspired name change).

The problem Moran faced when compiling his next published work, *Winston Churchill: the struggle for survival*, was that he sought to document his central character (Churchill) while casting himself as the hero; this involved him in an early example of the 'spin' that is now employed by advertising consultants and Blairite politicians. It was John Colville who observed that Moran was not even at the centre of many of the events where he is supposed to have been such an important figure – he would be invited to lunch the day after, and there told what had happened.[16]

But his most reprehensible action was to publish his so-called diary when and in the way he did. It is apparent from Lady Soames's biography of her mother just how selfish and inconsiderate Moran was when preparing to publish;[17] and his two main grounds for doing so at all seem to have been that G.M. Trevelyan urged him to do so, and that he needed the money because of all he had to give up during the war (for this was the story that gained wide currency and could hardly have originated other than with him).

Now the ethical and professional obligations of the social historian may well differ from those of a medical attendant; but in any case it is one thing to record medical information and quite another to offer an account of 'How I won the War'.

As for the plea of poverty, Moran and his family received numerous settlements from Churchill himself after (as Moran's own biographer records) he had declined an offer of a state stipend. The details of these settlements are recorded by Lady Soames in her biography of her mother;[17] and amid all the meanness I have had to record of Lord Moran himself, it is agreeable to find mentioned the 'charming and grateful letters' written by the Moran sons, John and Geoffrey, at the first renewal of their own settlements.

Equally agreeable was Lord Brain's tribute, in his letter to *The Times* in May 1966. Brain wrote to point out that 'controversial matters' in Moran's just-released book had been published without his knowledge, and to dispute the accuracy of some of Moran's recollections; but, being a gentleman, he did not go on to challenge Moran's snide remarks about his own personality and abilities, writing instead

May I say one thing more? I hope that this unhappy controversy will not be allowed to obscure Lord Moran's services to Sir Winston. Over the years I saw his devotion at first hand, and I know that it was given at great personal sacrifice. In addition Lord Moran has done much for medicine in this country.[18]

One of the illustrations in Lady Soames' biography of her mother is a photograph of Lord Moran. Its caption reads, 'His care and judgment, and his ability to summon specialised help from anywhere at any moment, were crucial to Winston's health.' At first reading, this is simply gracious; on closer examination, it raises the possibility that the author saw Moran as providing what would be called, these days, a call centre. I am informed that a protocol, among the Churchill familiars, ran thus: 'If he gets sick, you send for Lord Moran, and he will send for a doctor.'[19] Yet Moran himself was regarded as a competent doctor, who gave up a good deal of his life to look after Churchill; we might say that he served in both World Wars.

We are left, then, with a strange chimera of a man: a man whose physical courage was undoubted and was indeed recognised, yet who lacked the moral courage to enter into discussion with Lady Churchill about his publication plans. An eminent leader of his profession, yet one who elbowed aside Churchill's own general practitioner, Dr Kenneth Ward, upon his own appointment; a supposed diarist, whose diary proved to be no more than a literary device; the president of a Royal College, who betrayed patient confidentiality. A man whose nickname attests to his devious character: I believe that Pietro Annigoni, who painted Moran's presidential portrait for his Royal College, saw this quality in his subject.

So does the College itself. A discussion of the presidential portraits, in the College's own book on its memorabilia, comments on the flair with which Lord Dawson's portrait (by de Laszlo) captures his authority, and Lord Moran's his cunning, and goes on happily to recount 'the story (unverifiable)' of Sir Winston Churchill's remark on seeing the Annigoni – 'Just right, Moran: makes you look like a mediaeval poisoner.'[20] Michael Brain has recalled the occasion but not the 'unverifiable story':

47 In Lord Moran's presidential portrait at the College of Physicians, Pietro Annigoni has captured the qualities of his subject.

I was present on the occasion of the presentation and unveiling of the portrait in the Royal College of Physicians adjacent to Trafalgar Square... as my father as President arranged for Winston to become a Fellow to make the presentation. He smuggled me into the gallery! Later I was introduced to Winston and shook his hand. Nothing was said at the time nor did I hear of any comment from my father.[21]

At least Moran's celebrated patient achieved nine decades of life and, at the end, provided Moran with the opportunity of delivering bulletins to the gathered newsmen on the doorstep of 28 Hyde Park Gate. He included a photograph of the process as an illustration in his book.

48 Lord Moran delivers a medical bulletin to media representatives from the steps of the Churchill residence at 28 Hyde Park Gate.

It may have made up for Lady Churchill's refusal of permission for him to use the Orpen portrait.[22]

49 A copy of the Orpen portrait of Churchill is in the dining hall of Churchill College in Cambridge, where it gave daily encouragement to the author in 2006.

But the closing passage of the Moran account must be hailed as redemptive: describing Sir Winston's interment 'at Bladon in a country churchyard, in the stillness of a winter evening' he goes on:

> **In the presence of his family and a few friends, Winston Churchill was committed to English earth, which in his finest hour he had held inviolate.**[23]

* * *

Winston Churchill as I perceive him was a great man, who was buffeted by illness or injury throughout his life, but survived for those nine decades; who was beset also by criticism and often calumny through much of that time, but held on to save his country and arguably the world. He gained the affection of those who served him (even if he drove them to distraction at times), so that on his ninetieth birthday Sir Ian Jacob sent him this message:

Warmest congratulations from one whose finest hours were spent in your service.

As far back as 1931, when Churchill appeared to be in terminal political decline, Harold Nicolson wrote these words: 'He is a man who leads forlorn hopes, and when the hopes of England become forlorn, he will once again be summoned to leadership.' And Churchill, the supreme survivor, *was* summoned and *did* lead.

NOTES

1   Bonham Carter, V: *Winston Churchill as I knew him.* 1965; London, Collins. p.16.

2   Published in the *Sunday Despatch*, 30 June 1934.

3   As Churchill himself put it: 'My tastes are simple. I am easily satisfied with the best.' [Quoted in *The Dominion Post*, 7 October 2006: Indulgence, p.9 – 'Business of fizziness' (which is itself a quotation from Christian Pol-Roger)]

4   Richardson, C: *From Churchill's secret circle to the BBC – the biography of Sir Ian Jacob.* 1991; London: Brassey's.
'Prof' [Professor Lindemann, later Lord Cherwell] was renowned for carrying three items of equipment: a pocket slide rule, a miniature Galilean telescope, and a pocket torch.

5   Moran, p. 444-5.

6   James, W: *Barrel and book.* 1949: Melbourne, Georgian House. p. 41.

7   Montague Browne, A: *Long sunset.* 1995: London, Cassell. p.115.

8   Quoted in Coote, C R: *Sir Winston Churchill: a self-portrait.* 1954; London, Eyre & Spottiswoode. p. 22.

9   Gilbert [2004] p.317.

10   Asquith, as prime minister in 1914, had certain disabilities: a reluctance to take decisive action; a propensity to alcohol (though it was asserted by Bonar Law, the Tory leader, that 'Asquith, when drunk, can make a better speech than any of the rest of us when sober'); and a relationship with Clementine Churchill's cousin, a young woman named Venetia Stanley, with whom he was besotted and to whom he wrote a torrent of letters, confiding even state and military secrets. She did not betray his literary confidences, but by

marrying - quite without warning him - his junior colleague Edwin Montagu ('the Assyrian', Asquith used to call Montagu in confidential exchanges with her) she broke his heart and succeeded in destroying him as a political figure. One fortunate outcome of all this is that she kept most of Asquith's letters to her; and they provide a running commentary on Asquith's thought processes in those interesting times. In his book *In search of Churchill*, Martin Gilbert provides a fascinating account of the evening when Venetia's daughter, Judy Montagu, introduced him to these letters.

11 Soames, M. *Clementine Churchill* (revised and updated) 2002; London: Doubleday, p.50.

12 Johnson, P. *Churchill*. 2009; New York: Viking Penguin. p.114.

13 The First Sea Lord concerned was Prince Louis of Battenberg. The family changed its name to Mountbatten, and Prince Louis' son, also Louis, devoted his own naval career to achieving what his father had been denied. As Earl Mountbatten of Burma, Chief of Defence Staff 1958-65, he may be said to have succeeded.

14 This happens also to be the hand position routinely adopted in pronouncing a benediction in the Roman and Orthodox churches; this has led to the hypothesis that the practice may have grown up in imitation of an early Pope who had a Dupuytren contracture. In this context it is interesting that, in March 2013, Pope Francis could be observed, at his inauguration, to pronounce a benediction with his hand in the so-called 'position of rest' – the fingers progressively but mildly bent – rather than following routine. The hand position that he assumed closely resembles that of Adam in the Michelangelo ceiling of the Sistine Chapel, where the conclave had so recently met and elected Francis to the Papacy.

15 Montague Browne, A: (1995) p. 326.

16 Colville's comment is recorded in: (ed.) Wheeler-Bennett, J: *Action this day*. 1967; London: Macmillan. p.110

17 Soames, M: (2002). p.557.

18 Brain (2000) *op. cit.* p. 6. Moran [p.451] had written of Brain that 'he has a first-rate intelligence, but it is hidden behind a rather ordinary exterior' – which is hardly felicitous.

19 Montague Browne, A: (2011). *Personal recollection.*

20 Davenport, G, McDonald, I & Moss-Gibbons, C (eds): *The Royal College of Physicians and its Collections.* 2001; London: James & James. p.151. The Annigoni portrait is quite small, and in 2010 was to be seen in the gloom of the entrance lobby to the Council room.

21 Brain, M (2011). *Personal recollection.*

22 Beasley, A W: (2010): Churchill, Moran and the struggle for survival. *J R Coll Physicians Edinb* 40: 362-7. The unpleasantness between Lord Moran and Lady Churchill, and his fruitless attempt to publish the Orpen portrait, is described here.

22 Moran: (1966) p. 790.

ABBREVIATIONS

ADC   Aide-de-Camp
AF   Admiral of the Fleet
ATS   Auxiliary Territorial Service

BA   Bachelor of Arts
BBC   British Broadcasting Corporation
BMA   British Medical Association

CBE   Commander of the Most Excellent Order of the British Empire
CH   Companion of Honour
CIGS   Chief of the Imperial General Staff
C-in-C Commander-in-Chief
CMG   Companion of the Most Distinguished Order of St Michael & St George
CO   Commanding Officer
CT   Computerised [axial] tomography

DBE   Dame Commander of the Most Excellent Order of the British Empire
DM   Doctor of Medicine
DPM   Diploma of Psychological Medicine
DSO   Companion of the Distinguished Service Order

ENT   Ear, nose and throat surgery [Otorhinolaryngology]

FM   Field Marshal
FRCP   Fellow of the Royal College of Physicians
FRCS   Fellow of the Royal College of Surgeons
FRS   Fellow of the Royal Society

GBE   Knight [or Dame] Grand Cross of the Most Excellent Order of the British Empire
GCB   Knight Grand Cross of the Most Honourable Order of the Bath
GCIE   Knight Grand Commander of the Most Eminent Order of the Indian Empire
GCMG Knight Grand Cross of the Most Distinguished Order of St Michael & St George
GCSI   Knight Grand Commander of the Most Exalted Order of the Star of India
GCVO Knight [or Dame] Grand Cross of the Royal Victorian Order
GOC   General Officer Commanding
GOC-in-C General Officer Commanding-in-Chief
GPI   General paralysis of the insane

ICI   Imperial Chemical Industries
IRA   Irish Republican Army

KBE   Knight Commander of the Most Excellent Order of the British Empire
KCB   Knight Commander of the Most Honourable Order of the Bath
KCIE   Knight Commander of the Most Eminent Order of the Indian Empire
KCMG   Knight Commander of the Most Distinguished Order of St Michael & St George
KCSI   Knight Commander of the Most Exalted Order of the Star of India
KCVO   Knight Commander of the Royal Victorian Order
KG   Knight of the Most Noble Order of the Garter
KT   Knight of the Most Ancient and Most Noble Order of the Thistle

LDS	Licentiate in Dental Surgery
LL D	Doctor of Laws
LRCP	Licentiate of the Royal College of Physicians
MA	Master of Arts
M&B	May and Baker
MB BS	Bachelor of Medicine & Bachelor of Surgery (e.g. London, Australia)
MB ChB	Bachelor of Medicine & Bachelor of Surgery (e.g. Cambridge, Edinburgh, NZ)
MC	Military Cross
MD	Doctor of Medicine
MP	Member of Parliament
MRCS	Member of the Royal College of Surgeons
MRI	Magnetic resonance imaging
MS	Master of Surgery
	Manuscript
NATO	North Atlantic Treaty Organisation
NY	New York State
NZ	New Zealand
OM	Order of Merit
PA	Personal Assistant
PC	Privy Councillor
PhD	Doctor of Philosophy
PM	Prime Minister
POW	Prisoner of war
PPS	Principal Private Secretary
PRCP	President of the Royal College of Physicians
PRCS	President of the Royal College of Surgeons
RA	Royal Academician
RAF	Royal Air Force
RAMC	Royal Army Medical Corps
RCP	Royal College of Physicians (unless specified otherwise, understood to be 'of London')
RCS	Royal College of Surgeons (unless specified, understood 'of England')
RMA	Royal Military Academy, Woolwich
ScD	Doctor of Science
TIA	Transient ischaemic attack ['Mini-stroke']
UK	United Kingdom (of Great Britain & Northern Ireland)
US	United States (of America)
VC	Victoria Cross (it takes precedence over all other postnominal letters)
WAAF	Women's Auxiliary Air Force
WHO	World Health Organisation

DRAMATIS PERSONAE

Many figures flit in and out of this story of Churchill and his medical 'adventures'; some are not well known, others have become the dim ghosts of history. The brief biographical sketches provided here may help the reader to place these characters and to distinguish, for instance, between Harold Alexander and Alexander Cadogan, placing them apart from the other Alexander, A V, who was First Lord in 1929 and again in Churchill's wartime administration, and who became Earl Alexander of Hillsborough, while Harold [or 'Alex'] was Earl Alexander of Tunis.

* denotes cross-references.

A

ALEXANDER, Harold ['Alex'] [1891-1969] Field-Marshal Earl Alexander of Tunis. Harrow; Sandhurst; Irish Guards. MC 1915, DSO 1916. Supervised evacuation of Dunkirk 1940; Burma 1942; Commander-in-chief Middle East 1942, Mediterranean 1944. Governor-General of Canada 1946-52; minister of defence 1952-4 in 2nd Churchill term. KG 1946; GCB 1942; OM 1959; GCMG 1946. Eric Linklater's essay on him, published in *The art of adventure* [London, Macmillan 1947] has the ring of truth.

ASQUITH, Herbert Henry [1852-1928] Earl of Oxford and Asquith. City of London School; Balliol. Distinguished as a barrister; MP 1886; widowed 1891. Home secretary in 1892 Gladstone ministry. Remarried 1894 Margot née Tennant. Chancellor of the Exchequer 1905. Prime Minister 1908. Criticised for conduct of war and forced to resign December 1916. His Liberal party thereafter declined steadily, giving way to Labour as the voice of radical politics in Britain.

ASQUITH, Violet [1887-1969] Daughter of H H Asquith*, friend and confidante of Winston Churchill, and later also of Clementine*. Married [Sir] Maurice Bonham-Carter 1915; published *Winston Churchill as I knew him* [London, Eyre & Spottiswoode 1965]. DBE 1953. Life peeress as Baroness Asquith of Yarnbury 1964.

AUCHINLECK, Claude John Eyre [1884-1981] Field-Marshal. Wellington College, Berkshire; Sandhurst. Egypt & Mesopotamia, DSO 1917. Commander-in-Chief India 1941; replaced Wavell* as C-in-C Middle East 1941-2; combined this with command of 8th Army after Ritchie* 'burned out' in Rommel's 1942 offensive; withdrew to Alamein. Replaced by Alexander* and Montgomery*, reappointed C-in-C India. After independence criticised as being partial to Pakistan; asked to resign by Mountbatten, then viceroy. GCIE 1940. GCB 1945.

B

BALDWIN, Stanley [1867-1947] Earl Baldwin of Bewdley. Politician, three times Prime Minister. Harrow, Trinity College, Cambridge. The son of a Worcestershire ironmaster, he cultivated a bluff trustworthy image while destroying the Lloyd George* coalition in 1922, and professing Britain's preparedness (when in fact Britain was ill-prepared, and Baldwin aware of it) during Hitler's* rise in the 1930s. These activities brought him into conflict with Churchill, to the extent that the latter, invited to send Baldwin a message of goodwill on his 80th birthday, responded: 'I wish Stanley Baldwin no ill, but it would have been much better if he had never lived.'

BANKART, Blundell [1879-1951] Orthopaedic surgeon to the Royal National Orthopaedic Hospital and to Maida Vale Hospital. He studied the mechanics of recurrent dislocation of the shoulder, and devised an operation to stabilise the joint which, although demanding to perform accurately, had a low [5%] recurrence rate. He wrote this procedure up in 1923, and could therefore have been in a position to help Churchill had the latter felt himself sufficiently frustrated by his condition.

BATTENBERG, Prince Louis of [1854-1921] Born in Graz, Austria, the son of Prince Alexander of Hesse, he was naturalised and entered the Royal Navy in 1868. He had a distinguished career, becoming First Sea Lord in 1912. His naval career was destroyed by the wave of xenophobia that afflicted Britain at the outbreak of the First War, and he resigned in October 1914. In 1917 he renounced his German titles and was created Marquess of Milford Haven. His son, Lord Louis Mountbatten, set out to emulate his father, and had a brilliant if controversial career (becoming Earl Mountbatten of Burma) before being assassinated by the IRA in 1979.

BEAVERBROOK, William Maxwell Aitken, Lord [1879-1964] Newspaper proprietor and politician. Born in Canada, he came to England and became a Tory MP in 1910. He helped Lloyd George* supersede Asquith* as PM, and was raised to the peerage the following year. In 1918 he became Minister of Information. He acquired or launched a number of newspapers between the wars and held various ministerial posts (aircraft production, supply, Lord Privy Seal) in Churchill's wartime governments. Clementine* considered him one of Winston's 'foul weather friends' and found his influence disturbing over many years. They were reconciled in old age.

BEDFORD, (Davis) Evan [1898-1978]. Physician and cardiologist. MD London 1925; FRCP 1931. Hon MD Cairo 1944. Physician to the Middlesex and National Heart Hospitals. Brigadier, Consulting Physician to the Middle East Forces: in 1943 he was called in consultation by Lord Moran* when Churchill developed atrial fibrillation during an episode of pneumonia. A notable bibliophile, he presented his collection to the Royal College of Physicians of London in 1971; it is focused on cardiology, consists of 1112 items, comprehensively indexed, and forms a separate collection in the College's Dorchester Library.

BELL, Gertrude [1868-1926] Orientalist. Lady Margaret Hall, Oxford. In 1888 she was the first woman to obtain 1st class honours in modern history; she became a noted alpinist, traveller and archaeologist. In 1915 she was appointed to the Arab intelligence bureau in Cairo, and she held subsequent appointments in emergent Iraq. In 1921 she was one of Churchill's 'team' at the Cairo conference. She died in Baghdad where, in 1923, she had helped inaugurate a national museum.

BLAND-SUTTON, Sir John [1855-1936] Surgeon. He trained at the Middlesex Hospital and rose through the ranks of anatomy prosection and lecturing to become consulting surgeon. He travelled in the Middle East and wrote of his experiences there. Elected to the Council of the Royal College of Surgeons of England in 1910, he was president of the College 1923-25. He, and his widow, were generous benefactors to the College, several of their gifts deriving from the acquisitions of his Middle East journeyings. In 1929 he held office as president in the Association of Surgeons of Great Britain and Ireland, and in the Royal Society of Medicine. He was Rudyard Kipling's surgeon and, having many interests in common, they became close friends. Kipling's collection of medical books, which included much of Bland-Sutton's writings, was presented to the young Royal Australasian College of Surgeons at the suggestion of Alfred Webb-Johnson*, who was Bland-Sutton's Middlesex colleague and one of his successors in the presidency, and who had taken over Kipling's surgical care.

BOTHA, Louis [1962-1919] South African soldier and statesman. Brought up on a farm in the Orange Free State, he mobilised a burgher force at the time of the 1895 Jameson raid, and mustered a commando at Vryheid on the outbreak of war in 1899. He captured Churchill after the episode of the armoured train; he became commandant-general on Joubert's death in March 1900, and after defeat in June he resorted to guerrilla warfare until satisfied with the Vereeniging treaty in 1902. In 1907 he formed a ministry, and he headed the Transvaal delegation to the Union convention in 1908. He supported Smuts who became prime minister of the Union, and the two of them supported Britain in 1914. The following year he led the campaign which secured German South-West Africa [now Namibia].

BRACKEN, Brendan Rendall [1901-58] Born in Ireland, he absconded from Jesuit College in Mungret and was sent to Australia. Returning to England in 1919, he became first a teacher, then went into publishing. He entered parliament in 1929 and became a loyal supporter of Churchill during the 'locust years' before serving as his Principal Private Secretary 1939-41 and then as minister of information until 1945, when he was briefly First Lord. He was made viscount in 1952, and was a generous benefactor of Churchill College, Cambridge. His loyalty and his red hair gave rise to the myth that he was Churchill's offspring.

BRAIN, Walter Russell, Lord Brain [1895-1966] Physician (neurologist) and medical statesman. New College, Oxford and the London Hospital. DM 1925, FRCP 1931. He succeeded Lord Moran* as president of the Royal College of Physicians of London 1950-57; he was knighted 1952, made baronet two years later, baron 1962 and FRS 1964. He edited the neurological journal, *Brain*, from 1954 until his death. He saw Churchill in consultation on a number of occasions; he was offended by Moran's misinterpretation of his opinions.

BRAINE, FW & CC. This father-and-son team, Francis Woodhouse and Charles Carter, were pioneers of dental anaesthesia, who attended young Churchill when, in 1891, he had to have a tooth extracted under general anaesthesia.

BROOK, Norman Craven [!902-67] Baron Normanbrook. Cabinet secretary. Wolverhampton Grammar School, Wadham College, Oxford. Entered civil service 1925. PPS to Sir John Anderson (later Viscount Waverley) 1938-42; secretary of the Cabinet 1947-62. In this capacity facilitated use of Cabinet documents in Churchill Second War histories. Chairman of governors, BBC 1964-67. GCB 1951; PC 1953; baron 1963.

BROOKE, Alan Francis [1993-1963] Field Marshal Viscount Alanbrooke. GCB 1942; KG 1946; OM 1946. Educated in France and at RMA, Woolwich. Service in Ireland and India pre-war; Western Front 1914-18. DSO and bar. Commander-in-Chief Southern Command 1939; in France as corps commander 1940; then C-in-C Home Forces. Chief of Imperial General Staff 1941; and Chairman of chiefs of staff committee 1941-45. In this post he was a constant observer of Churchill as PM; his diaries, edited by Arthur Bryant, stirred some controversy because of their candour, but beneath the candour he wrote of his wartime chief, 'He is quite the most wonderful man I have ever met.'

BUTTLE, Gladwin Albert Hurst OBE. b.1899. MRCS LRCP 1924, MA Cambridge 1927. As transfusion officer attached to 15 Scottish Hospital in North African campaigns, he became an acknowledged expert also in the administration of sulphonamides, developed by the British firm May and Baker, and in their time the 'wonder drug' for treatment of infections. He was called in to supervise the use of 'M&B' for the treatment of Churchill's pneumonia in December 1943. After the war he was Wellcome professor in the pharmacy school of the University of London and, when Macmillan* published his diaries in 1984, emeritus professor at Bart's.

BUZZARD, Dr Thomas. Neurologist, called in consultation by Dr Roose* when Lord Randolph Churchill's* mental condition deteriorated in 1892. Lord Randolph declined a second consultation in 1894, but his disorder worsened during a world tour to the extent that he had to be restrained in a strait-jacket at Colombo and brought back to London. Here, alarmed by the news of his condition, the Prince of Wales (later King Edward VII) had his own doctor ask Buzzard the nature of the disease. Buzzard replied: 'Lord Randolph is affected with "General Paralysis" the early symptoms of which… were evident to me at an interview two years ago.' In recent years doubt has been cast on the diagnosis; but no firm (as opposed to conjectural) alternative is established.

C

CADOGAN, Alexander George Montagu [1884-1968] Diplomat. Eton and Balliol. Entered diplomatic service 1908. Head of League of Nations section 1921-33. Minister in Peking 1934-35. Permanent under-secretary 1938-46. British representative at United Nations 1946-50. Chairman BBC 1952-57. KCB 1941; GCMG 1939; PC 1946; OM 1951. His war diaries were published posthumously in 1971.

CHAMBERLAIN, Neville [1869-1940] Politician. Son of Joseph, half-brother of Sir Austen, Chamberlain. Rugby School. First distinguished himself as a local body politician in Birmingham; entered parliament in 1918 and, after holding numerous ministerial posts, succeeded Baldwin* in 1937. He continued the policy of appeasement which had encouraged Hitler's aggression, returning from Munich with the promise of 'peace in our time'. In May 1940 he accepted the inevitable and resigned in favour of Churchill but (perhaps because he was sincerely misguided, whereas Baldwin was merely manipulative) Churchill retained his respect for Chamberlain and kept him in a Cabinet post until his final illness.

CHANNON, Sir Henry ['Chips'] [1897-1958] Born in Chicago, grandson of a migrant from Somerset who became a prosperous shipowner. In 1917 Henry returned to France where he had been educated, as a member of the American Red Cross, and in !918 he settled permanently in England. In 1933 he married Lady Honor Guinness, eldest daughter of the 2nd Earl of Iveagh; the marriage lasted 12 years, but saw him into the safe parliamentary seat of Southend-on-Sea. He was knighted in 1957. He entertained the royal and the rich, and his diaries, published in 1967, provided a wealth of cheerful gossip and some shrewd observation.

CHURCHILL, Clarissa [1920-] Daughter of John [Jack] Churchill*, niece of Winston. She became the second wife of Anthony Eden*; they were married on 14 August 1952, the reception being held at No 10 Downing Street. She became Countess of Avon with Eden's peerage in 1961.

CHURCHILL, Clementine [née Hozier] [1885-1977] Wife of Winston (they were married on 12 September 1908; they nicknamed one another: 'Cat' and 'Pig' and these terms of affection were as durable as their marriage.) A remarkable woman, who subordinated her own wishes and ambitions to support her husband's career, but without ever becoming submissive. When the Russians became Britain's allies she inaugurated an Aid to Russia Fund, and in 1945 she travelled extensively in the Soviet Union, doing much to thaw relations. Made CBE in 1918, she was promoted GBE on 1946, on the recommendation of the Labour government that had displaced her husband the previous year. The Russians had awarded her the Order of the Red Banner of Labour in 1945. She received a life peerage in 1965, becoming Baroness Spencer-Churchill.

CHURCHILL, Diana [1909-63] Eldest daughter of Winston and Clementine*. She married first John Bailey, and second Duncan Sandys; but both marriages ended in divorce. She took her own life.

CHURCHILL, John Spencer [Jack] [1880-1947] Younger brother of Winston. Stockbroker. Married Lady Gwendoline Bertie (nicknamed 'Goonie'). Served in South Africa, wounded; 1914-18 France and at Gallipoli. In 1929 the brothers travelled, with their sons (Randolph* and Johnnie) through Canada and the US; they dubbed themselves the 'Churchill troupe'.

CHURCHILL, Randolph Henry Spencer: Lord Randolph [1849-95] Father of Winston, third son of the 7th Duke of Marlborough*. Eton and Merton College, Oxford. In 1874, the year of Winston's birth, he became Conservative MP for Woodstock; but he was soon playing a gadfly role in his party. He visited India in 1884, and became secretary of state for India the following year; in 1886 he became Chancellor of the Exchequer, but he resigned rather than compromise on a controversial budget, and so brought his political career to a premature close. His relations with his son were mostly coloured by his incessant criticism, but he established himself in young Winston's mind as a model to be emulated. He became aggressively insane in the period leading up to his death; the cause was more plain to his doctors then, than to some later students of his condition.

CHURCHILL, Lady Randolph [Jennie Jerome] [1854-1921] Mother of Winston; daughter of Leonard* and Clara Jerome*. She and her two sisters were living with their mother in Paris when, during Cowes Week in 1873, she and Lord Randolph Churchill* met and promptly fell in love. They were married at the British Embassy in Paris on 15 April 1874, and her first son was born prematurely on 30 November that year; his prematurity took the Blenheim establishment by surprise. Widowed at the age of 41, she remarried twice, on each occasion choosing a husband of about that son's age. In 1900 she married George Cornwallis-West; they were divorced in 1913; her third husband was Montague Porch, who gave up his job with the Nigerian civil service and gave her the company she craved. But that was a brief if happy marriage: in 1921 she died of complications following an ankle fracture.

CHURCHILL, Mary: see SOAMES, Lady

CHURCHILL, Randolph Spencer [1911-68] Son of Winston. Eton and (briefly) Christ Church, Oxford. He suffered from the disability of being the son of a famous father, which dogged his attempts at a political career (these in turn embarrassed his father); it brought a touch of comedy to his military service, which was otherwise creditable. He was twice married, and twice divorced. He became his father's official biographer, with Martin Gilbert* as his assistant and, after Randolph's early death, his successor in this task; Gilbert's account of their association, in *In search of Churchill*, is a sympathetic study of a man who was almost distinguished.

CHURCHILL, Sarah [1911-82] ['Mule'] Second daughter of Winston and Clementine*. She pursued a stage career, and in 1936 she married her fellow-actor Vic Oliver. The marriage lasted for five years, and after it broke down she joined the WAAF, serving quite often as an informal ADC to her father. Her second husband was the photographer Anthony Beauchamp; they married in 1949, but this marriage too was doomed and in 1957 he took his own life. In 1962, after a turbulent period, she made a happy marriage with Henry, the 23rd Baron Audley, only to be widowed when he suffered a fatal heart attack the following year.

COCKCROFT, Sir John (Douglas) [1897-1967] Physicist. Victoria University, Manchester, and St John's College, Cambridge. Research student under Ernest Rutherford at Cavendish Laboratory 1924-39; work on radar with Sir Henry Tizard 1938-40; head of the Air Defence Research and Development Establishment, 1940-43; in charge of Montreal laboratory and the building of NRX heavy water reactor at Chalk River, Canada 1943-46. Director of Atomic Energy Research Station, Harwell 1946-59. First Master of Churchill College, Cambridge, 1959-67. Nobel Prize for Physics 1951. KCB 1953, OM 1957.

COLLINS, Michael [1890-1922] A leader of the Irish revolutionary movement, one of five who took part in negotiations with Churchill that resulted in a settlement. Born in Co. Cork, he worked in London 1906-16, becoming an active member of the Irish Republican Brotherhood. He returned to Ireland and took part in the Easter Rebellion, being briefly imprisoned. After the 1921 settlement he became chairman and minister of finance in the provisional Irish government, and when civil war broke out in June 1922 he reduced the opposition in Dublin, before being assassinated by irregulars.

COLVILLE, Sir John ['Jock'] [1915-1987] Harrow; Trinity College, Cambridge. He was a page of honour to King George V, his mother being one of Queen Mary's ladies-in-waiting. He joined the diplomatic service in 1937, and two years later was transferred to 10 Downing Street as an assistant private secretary to Neville Chamberlain*. In May 1940 Churchill inherited him 'with the other livestock'. He served a couple of years with the RAF before being recalled to No 10. In 1947 he became Private Secretary to the then Princess Elizabeth, and the following year he married her lady-in-waiting, Lady Margaret Egerton. He returned briefly to the Foreign Service and a posting to Lisbon, before Churchill, on regaining office in 1951, claimed his services again. After Churchill's retirement in 1955, Colville entered the world of banking and also took to writing; but his great achievement about this time was to sow the seed of what became Churchill College. His knighthood in 1974 reflected this achievement; and the meeting hall in the Archives Centre bears his name.

COX, Sir Percy (Zachariah) [1864-1937] Administrator And diplomat. Harrow and Sandhurst. Joined Indian Staff Corps 1889. Various postings about the Red Sea 1893-1914. In 1909 secured lease of land fronting on Euphrates for Anglo-Persian Oil Company. Chief political officer, Indian Expeditionary Force in Mesopotamia 1914-18; negotiated treaty with Ibn Saud 1915. High Commissioner to Iraq 1920-23. KCIE 1909, KCSI 1915, GCIE 1917, GCMG 1922.

CUNNINGHAM, Andrew Browne, Viscount Cunningham of Hyndhope [1883 1963] Admiral of the Fleet. Son of Daniel Cunningham, professor of anatomy Dublin and Edinburgh. Edinburgh Academy; cadetship in *Britannia* 1897. Commissioned lieutenant 1904. Commanded destroyer *Scorpion* 1911-18: Dardanelles 1915, DSO; Dover Patrol, bars to DSO 1919, 1920. Commanded battleship *Rodney* 1929; Battlecruiser Squadron 1937-38. Commander-in-Chief Mediterranean 1939; Taranto 1940; Cape Matapan 1941. Naval commander for North African landings 1942. First Sea Lord 1943-45. GCB 1941; KT 1945; OM 1946. Lord Rector, Edinburgh University 1945-48. Lord High Commissioner to the General Assembly of the Church of Scotland 1950, 1952.

D

DABBS, Dr G H R. Medical practitioner, novelist, playwright, horse-breeder. He communicated with Churchill's friend and colleague Jack Seely*, offering a cheerful prognosis after Churchill's disturbing lapse of concentration during a speech in Parliament in 1904.

D'ABERNON, Viscount (Vincent, Sir Edgar) [1857-1941] Financier and diplomat. Eton. Coldstream Guards 1877-82. Financial adviser to Egyptian government 1883-89. KCMG 1887. Governor, Imperial Ottoman Bank 1889-97. Chairman, Royal Commission on Imperial Trade 1912. Baron 1914. GCMG, 1917; PC, and appointed ambassador to Berlin 1920. Viscount and GCB 1926; FRS 1934. Distinguished in his own right, he is principally remembered for his lyrical account of the impression created by Lady Randolph Churchill* as a young woman.

DAVIDSON, Henry. Assistant master of Harrow School, who complained to Lady Randolph of her son Winston's 'forgetfulness, carelessness, unpunctuality and irregularity in every way,' in a letter dated 12 July 1888.

DAWSON, Bertrand Edward [1864-1945] Viscount Dawson of Penn. Physician. St Paul's School; University College, London. BSc 1888, qualified in Medicine 1890. Physician to London Hospital 1906-45. KCVO 1911, GCVO 1917. Consulting Physician in France 1914-1919; physician-in-ordinary to George V from 1914. Dealt with king's injuries when thrown by horse while inspecting troops in France 1915. At urging of Lloyd George (and despite king's reservations about apparent favouritism) awarded peerage 1920. Saw Churchill in consultation at time of appendicitis 1922. Drew pus off king's empyema 1928, subsequent open drainage [by Sir Hugh Rigby] and ultimate recovery. Attended George V in his final illness; composed bulletin (apparently on the back of a menu card): 'The King's life is moving peacefully towards its close.' President RCP London 1931-38; viscount 1936.

DE GASPERI, Alcide [1881-1954] Prime Minister of Italy 1945-53. Born in Trentino, studied at Innsbruck and Vienna; entered parliament 1911; imprisoned by Mussolini as anti-fascist in 1927. Worked in the Vatican library from 1929 until he became prime minister of newly-republican Italy. Churchill's dinner guest on 23 June 1953, the evening of Churchill's second major stroke.

DE VALERA, Eamon [1882-1975] Irish politician. Brought up on a farm in Co. Limerick, he became a teacher and was active in a variety of Republican movements. He took part in the 1916 uprising and was lucky to escape the firing squad. In 1917 he became an MP, leading Sinn Fein 1917-26 and opposing the 1921 settlement. His Republican party won the 1932 election and he served as prime minister for three terms: 1932-48, 1951-54 and 1957-59, when he became president, serving until 1973.

DILL, Sir John (Greer) [1881-1944] Field marshal. Cheltenham and Sandhurst. South Africa 1901. Brigade major 1914; various staff appointments, DSO 1917. Instructor Imperial Defence College 1926-29; commandant Staff College 1931-34. Palestine 1936-37; commanded 1 Corps in France 1939-40. Chief of Imperial General Staff May 1940. Field-marshal 1941; when health deteriorated resigned CIGS appointment; visited US with Churchill December 1941, and remained as senior British representative on chiefs of staff committee in Washington until his death. GCB 1942. He gained the respect of his US colleagues and was buried in Arlington cemetery.

DORMAN-SMITH, Eric [Eric Dorman O'Gowan] Major-General, MC: soldier and litigant. He was Auchinleck's Deputy Chief of General Staff in 1942, and was 'relieved' of this post as part of the reshuffle when his chief was replaced by Alexander*. When Churchill's fourth volume of war memoirs, *The hinge of fate*, was published a decade later, Dorman-Smith (now living in his native Ireland, and calling himself Dorman O'Gowan) initiated an action for libel, claiming that the mention – in a telegram from Churchill to Attlee and the war cabinet dated 6 August 1942 – of his being relieved, set against a Churchill telegram to the War Cabinet on 21 August which read 'I am sure we were heading for disaster under the former regime', served to 'spread the story of his incompetence to the ends of the earth'. The matter was ultimately resolved on the basis of a promise to exculpate Dorman-Smith in a footnote to future printings of the volume in question. O'Gowan was a leading source for Corelli Barnett's 1960 appraisal of *The desert generals*.

DUNHILL, Sir Thomas (Peel) [1876-1957] Surgeon. Australian-born, and raised by a widowed mother in rural Victoria, Dunhill worked as a pharmacist for six years before being able to begin a medical course in 1899. His undergraduate career was outstanding and marked the beginnings of his lifelong interest in thyroid disease. By 1906 he had acquired an MD, and gained a surgical appointment. In the First War he went with the Australian forces to Egypt and then to France, where he was to become Consulting Surgeon to the British Army and gain a CMG. He also came to the eye of George Gask of Bart's and, in 1920 when he was settling back into Melbourne, Gask recruited him to the newly established professorial unit at Bart's. He became surgeon to the Royal Household and KCVO, and a prominent figure on the surgical scene in London. He was advanced to GCVO in 1949. He was the surgeon appointed to operate on Churchill's hernia in 1947.

E

EDEN, (Robert) Anthony [1897-1977] 1st Earl of Avon. Statesman. Eton; King's Royal Rifle Corps 1915. MC 1917; youngest brigade major in British Army 1918. Christ Church, Oxford 1919 [1st in oriental languages, 1922] Conservative MP for Warwick and Leamington 1923-57. PPS to Foreign Secretary 1926; Lord Privy Seal 1933; Minister for League of Nations affairs, Foreign secretary after resignation of Sir Samuel Hoare 1935; was in favour of appeasement when Chamberlain* became PM in 1937, but Lord Halifax's visit to Hitler, and Chamberlain's rejection of a Roosevelt* proposal without consultation soured their relationship. Eden resigned 1938 and was replaced by Halifax. Minor posts until 1940, then Foreign secretary again until 1945. Third term 1951-55, then succeeded Churchill as Prime Minister, having been eager to do so for some years. Was by now suffering the effects of a botched gall bladder operation, which necessitated two further operations, the final one in US; mishandled the response to Nasser's nationalisation of the Suez canal in 1956 and the British-French assault, represented as a response to the Israeli attack on Egypt, was highly successful in military terms but defeated by US pressure. Resigned 1957. PC 1934; KG 1954; Peerage 1961.

EDWARDS, Harold Clifford CBE. Surgeon. Graduated 1923, FRCS 1926, MS 1928. Jacksonian prize, RCS 1932. Surgeon, King's College Hospital, and director of surgical studies, King's College Hospital Medical School. Brigadier RAMC and consulting surgeon to Middle East Forces 1945: called in by Lord Moran* to see Churchill about his hernia; prescribed truss. Member of Council, Royal College of Surgeons of England, 1955-71, and a vice-president 1967-69.

EISENHOWER, Dwight David ['Ike'] [1890-1969] Soldier, later President of US. Born in Texas of German immigrant stock; trained at West Point and by 1939 was chief military assistant to General McArthur in the Philippines. Was designated commander for operation Torch, the Allied landings in North Africa, 1942, his first combat experience. He proved himself a skilful coordinator of multinational forces, and was chosen as commander for 'Overlord', the Normandy landings in 1944. He became Supreme Commander of NATO Land Forces in 1950, and was elected president of the US in 1952 and again in 1956. He pursued a campaign against Communism but would not risk an attempt to achieve détente.

ENGLISH, Sir [Thomas] Crisp [1878-1949]. Surgeon. Westminster and St George's. LRCP 1900, MB London 1903, BS 1904. FRCS 1903. Descended from a North Yorkshire family, he was the son of TJ English, who practised in South Kensington and was anaesthetist to the Cancer [now Royal Marsden] Hospital. He had a distinguished academic career – Murchison scholar of the RCP 1900, Jacksonian prizeman of RCS 1902, Hunterian professor 1904. Commissioned into RAMC 1913; BEF France, Colonel 1917; thereafter Salonika and North Italy fronts. CMG 1917, KCMG 1918. Knighthoods in Orders of St Sava [Servia], George I [Greece] and St John. Surgeon to St George's, and also Queen Alexandra's Hospital, Millbank, Royal Hospital, Chelsea and King Edward VII's Hospital for Officers. Operated on Churchill for appendicitis in 1922.

EVEREST, Mrs Anne ['Oom', 'Woom', or 'Woomany'] Churchill's nurse (or nanny): it was she who, in effect, brought him up and made good the deficiencies in his parents' support. As a result he was as devoted to her as she had been to him. When Lady Randolph* decided in 1891 to dispense with her services, Winston's concern led to her being appointed to the household of the Duchess of Marlborough*. She died in 1895.

F

FERGUSSON, Bernard Edward [1911-80] 1st Lord Ballantrae. Soldier, author, governor-general. Son of Sir Charles Fergusson, grandson of Sir James Fergusson and of Lord Glasgow, all three of them past holders of vice-regal office in New Zealand. Eton and Sandhurst; commissioned into Black Watch 1931. ADC to General Wavell* 1935; commanded Chindit column in Burma 1943, and 16 Brigade in the 1944 campaign. Palestine Police 1946-47. Commanded 1st Battalion The Black Watch in Germany 1948-51. Allied Force HQ during Suez operation 1956. Commanded 29 Infantry Brigade 1957-58. DSO OBE. Governor-General of New Zealand 1962-67. GCMG 1962; GCVO 1963. Wrote books on his two Chindit campaigns; the history of Combined Operations, *The watery maze*; the short biography *Wavell – portrait of a soldier*; and sundry reminiscences. Like Andrew Cunningham* he served as Lord High Commissioner (the Queen's representative) at the General Assembly of the Church of Scotland and, again like Cunningham, he was awarded the Thistle, in 1974. [It is interesting that the New Zealand connexion was extended into a fourth generation when his son George Fergusson became British High Commissioner in 2006.]

FISH, Sir (Eric) Wilfred CBE. Dentist, who looked after Churchill over a number of years. He qualified in dentistry [LDS] in 1914, and in medicine [MB ChB] two years later. He achieved an MD from Manchester in 1924, a London DSc in 1933, and was made DDSc by Melbourne University in 1935. He was on the staff of St Mary's Hospital and later honorary Director of the department of Dental Science at the Royal College of Surgeons. He was chairman of the General Dental Council. Many other distinctions were bestowed on this leader of an emerging profession.

FRANKLIN, Hugh. Supporter of the Suffragette movement, who attacked Churchill with a whip in the course of a train journey from Bradford to London in 1910.

FRENCH, Sir John (Denton Pinkstone) [1852-1925] 1st Earl of Ypres. Field marshal. Joined the Royal Navy in 1866, but transferred to the army in 1874. He distinguished himself in the Sudan in 1884-85 and in South Africa 1899-1901. He was Chief of the Imperial General Staff 1911-14, and was commander-in-chief of the British Expeditionary Force in France 1914-15; but his performance attracted such criticism that he resigned at the end of 1915 and was replaced by Haig. He was Lord-Lieutenant of Ireland 1918-22.

FREYBERG, Bernard (Cyril) [1889-1963] 1st Baron Freyberg of Wellington NZ and Munstead in Surrey. Soldier, governor-general. Born in Richmond-upon-Thames; brought to NZ as a two-year-old. Attended Wellington College NZ, where he achieved distinction as a swimmer, winning national titles as a youth. Trained as a dentist. Travelled to England in 1914, arriving just after outbreak of War. Royal Naval Division: Antwerp, Gallipoli. Won first DSO for swimming ashore and planting decoy flares, night before landings. Twice wounded. France 1916: VC at Beaucourt, and wounded again. Passchendaele, wounded. Ended war as brigadier-general. Obtained regular commission in Grenadier Guards; reached rank of major-general, then discharged on medical grounds 1937. In Second War commanded 2nd NZ Expeditionary Force in Greece, Crete, North Africa and Italy; 1946-52 governor-general of New Zealand. 1953 Lieutenant Governor and Deputy Constable of Windsor Castle. GCMG KBE DSO and 3 bars. He was Churchill's friend from 1914.

G

GARNETT, Theresa. Suffragette: attacked Churchill with a dog-whip on a railway station in 1909; when he grasped her wrists she attempted to push him under moving train. Clementine intervened and stopped him from being driven over the edge of the platform.

GILBERT, Sir Martin [b. 1936] PC CBE DLitt. Historian. Highgate School and Magdalen College, Oxford. Became research assistant to Randolph Churchill* on official biography 1962, and succeeded him in 1968. Produced official biography [six of the 8 volumes] and 11 volumes (to date) of associated documents; has written a 'short' Churchill biography, *Churchill – a life*; an account of the detective work involved in the official biography, *In search of Churchill*; and most recently *Churchill and America*. His other books include *First Wold War*, *Second World War*, the *Battle of the Somme* and *D-Day*. He is also an authority on the Holocaust. In 2009 he was appointed to the British government's inquiry, headed by Sir John Chilcot, into Britain's policy on Iraq 2001-9.

GOTT, William Henry Ewart ['Strafer'] [1897-1942] Soldier. Harrow and Sandhurst. Commissioned into King's Royal Rifle Corps 1915. POW 1917. Battalion commander in Egypt 1938-39; rose to command 7 Armoured Division in 1941. Churchill had selected him to command 8th Army in the reshuffle of August 1942, but his aircraft was shot down as he was taking off for a short leave before assuming his new appointment. [It was this that gave Montgomery* his big chance.] DSO & bar, 1941; CB 1942.

GRIFFITH, Arthur [1872-1922] Irish political leader. He became part of the nationalist movement at a young age; he worked in the Transvaal 1896-99, then returned to Ireland and founded a weekly newspaper, *The united Irishman*. Advocated Sinn Fein ('ourselves alone') policy and became president of that party 1910. He was not part of the Easter rising in 1916, but was imprisoned on occasions thereafter. Passed presidency to de Valera* 1917, but acting president 1919-20. In 1921 he and Michael Collins* led the delegation which achieved a settlement in talks with Churchill. He became president of Dail Eireann in 1922.

GUEST, Alice [1880-1948] Churchill's cousin's wife: Lord Randolph's* sister Cornelia married Ivor Bertie Guest, and their son Ivor Churchill Guest (who became Viscount Wimborne) married Alice Grosvenor. It was at dinner with the Guests in 1911 that Alice told Churchill of 'her doctor in Germany, who completely cured her depression'.

H

HEBERDEN, William [1710-1801] Physician, commonly called 'the elder' to distinguish him from his son and namesake, who was also a physician of note. He graduated BA from St John's College, Cambridge in 1728, and MD in 1759, having become FRCP in 1746 and FRS three years later. He was the first to describe angina pectoris, though he did not appreciate that it resulted from inadequacy of the coronary circulation. His *Commentaries*, which were written for the guidance of his son and (at his own request) published only after his death, contain his account of the condition.

HITLER, Adolf [1889-1945] Dictator. An Austrian native, he was born in Braunau, and destined by his father for the civil service. But after his father died in 1903, he sought to pursue a career as an artist. He lived a hand-to-mouth existence, evading national service in the Austrian army, until he moved to Munich in 1913 and found employment as a draughtsman. He joined the German army in 1914 and became a corporal in a Bavarian regiment; he was wounded by gas at the time of the armistice. In the 1920s he became an agitator against the terms of the treaty of Versailles, and built round himself the National Socialist German Workers' [or 'Nazi'] party; he was defeated in the presidential elections of 1932, but became chancellor the following year. He discarded constitutional restraints and trampled on opposition, burning the Reichstag building in 1933 and denouncing the arson as a Communist plot. Thereafter he rearmed Germany, occupied the Rhineland, occupied Austria at the beginning of 1938 and (in two bites) Czechoslovakia within the next year, fobbing off Chamberlain* at Munich in the process. Only when, in September 1939, he invaded Poland did Britain and France act in accord with the guarantees they had given. In June 1941 Hitler invaded Russia, with whom he had made an alliance two years earlier; but Russian courage and the winter snows combined to repel him after his early victories in the East. Thereafter his cause did not prosper and in April 1945, in a bunker under his besieged capital, Berlin, he committed suicide.

HUNTER, John [1728-93] Surgeon. The youngest child of a Lanarkshire farmer, John grew up a rebellious child, curious about natural history and quite unimpressed by formal learning. At the age of 20 he brought himself to London and became an assistant in the anatomy school of his older brother William. He had found his vocation and, studying under Cheselden and Pott, two of the leading surgeons of the day, he himself became a surgeon. He served as an army surgeon at Belleisle and in Portugal during the Seven Years' War (in his spare time he began to collect specimens to illustrate his belief in the interdependence of structure and function in living things), then returned to London where he was surgeon to St George's Hospital and became the leading surgeon of his own generation. His collection (though damaged by the activities of his brother-in-law and executor, Everard Home, and a century later by German bombing) is the jewel in the crown of the Royal College of Surgeons of England, and under the care of the Hunterian Trustees, whose bicentenary was celebrated in 1999. Hunter's remains are in Westminster Abbey, where his memorial brass identifies him as 'the founder of scientific surgery'.

I

INSKIP, Thomas Walker Hobart [1876-1947] Lawyer and politician. Clifton and King's College, Cambridge. Called to the bar 1899; KC 1914. Naval intelligence 1914-18; then became a Conservative MP. Knighted 1922; variously solicitor-general and attorney-general 1922-36. Was then appointed Minister for Co-ordination of Defence, a post which might more appropriately have gone to Churchill. Became Viscount Caldecote in 1939. Served as lord chief justice 1940-46.

J

JENNER, Edward [1749-1823] Pioneer of vaccination for smallpox. He was a favourite pupil of John Hunter* with whom thereafter he kept up a correspondence; his sorting of specimens brought back from Cook's first voyage led to his being proposed as naturalist for the second, but he preferred to return to his native Berkeley in Gloucestershire and practise as a country GP. Here he observed that milkmaids who got cowpox did not have their complexions (indeed their lives) put at risk by smallpox. This led him to develop the procedure of vaccination, in which lymph from an affected calf was introduced under the skin. An astute observer, Jenner made the link between coronary artery disease and angina.

JEROME, Clara, née Hall [1825-95] Mother of Lady Randolph Churchill*. She was the daughter of Ambrose Hall, a member of the New York State Assembly, and Anna, née Baker, who is believed to have had Amerindian ancestry. She and her husband Leonard* had three daughters, Clarita, Jennie and Leonie, a fourth having died young; and in 1867 she took the three girls to live in Paris. Her husband used to come over to France in the winter, and they would go to a spa town, Pau, in the Pyrenees. In 1871 they went to Cowes on the Isle of Wight to watch the yachting of Cowes Week; two years later Mrs Jerome took her daughters back to Cowes, and it was here that Jennie met Lord Randolph.

JEROME, Leonard [1818-91] American businessman, father of Lady Randolph.* After his marriage in 1849 he lived in Rochester, in upstate New York, where he bought the town's principal newspaper. He and his wife moved to New York City the following year, where he became a successful stockbroker; in 1851 he was appointed American consul in Trieste, serving two years before a political changeover saw him replaced. He returned to New York to find that a brother, left in charge of the family firm, had caused it to fail; he had restored its fortunes by 1854 when Jennie, the future Lady Randolph, was born. In 1858 Jerome bought a large interest in the *New York Times*; he was an active supporter of the Union in the Civil War, and, in 1866, he and his brother Lawrence built a racecourse, Jerome Park: he has been called 'the father of American horseracing'. He 'had an eye for the ladies,' and it is reported that his wife remarked to one of his mistresses, 'I feel so sorry for you, my dear: he really is irresistible.'

K

KITCHENER, Horatio Herbert [1850-1916] Field marshal. Royal Military Academy, Woolwich; commissioned in Royal Engineers 1871. He served in Lord Wolseley's relief expedition aimed at rescuing General Gordon 1884-5; he remained in Egypt and became Sirdar of the Egyptian Army in 1892, preparing to clear the dervish forces out of the Sudan. This campaign culminated in the battle of Omdurman in 1898 where, in spite of Kitchener's strenuous efforts to avoid having him, young Churchill managed to take part in the cavalry charge of the 21st Lancers. In the South African war he became chief of staff to Lord Roberts in 1899; as commander-in-chief 1900-02 he had to deal with prolonged guerrilla activity on the part of the Boers. He was a reforming commander-in-chief in India 1902-09, British agent in Egypt in 1911 and, in 1914, became War Minister in the Asquith* Cabinet. He was a difficult colleague but did oversee the build-up of Britain's army from 20 to 70 divisions; he was lost in the sinking of HMS *Hampshire* while on his way to Russia. KCMG 1894; KCB 1896; OM 1902; KG 1915.

KYNNERSLEY, H W Sneyd. Headmaster of St George's School, Ascot, which Churchill entered at the age of 7. The boy's first acquaintance with his headmaster (whose sadism is well documented in Anne Sebba's *Jennie Churchill*) was when his three half-crowns were handed over and 'duly entered in a book'; thereafter he 'experienced the fullest applications of the secular arm' in the form of the floggings which complemented 'frequent religious services of a somewhat High Church character in the chapel'. In *My early life* Churchill records that he 'fell into a low state of health' at the school, which he misnames, perhaps deliberately, St James's.

L

LAVERY, Sir John [1856-1941] Painter. Born in Belfast, he studied at the Glasgow School of Art, and was influenced by Whistler and the Impressionists. He painted Queen Victoria's visit to the Glasgow Exhibition in 1888, and his success thereafter was unabated. He was knighted in 1918, and made RA in 1921. He painted Churchill in uniform, in his French-pattern steel helmet, but of more significance he and his wife Hazel (who was an accomplished artist in her own right) did much to encourage Churchill's own career as a painter. It was Hazel who emboldened his brushwork when he first attempted to paint in oils, and did much to provide him with 'diversional therapy' after the Dardanelles imbroglio.

LAWRENCE, Thomas Edward ['Lawrence of Arabia'] [1888-1935] Arabist, scholar, soldier. Born in Tremadoc in Wales, he graduated with a 1st class degree in modern history from Jesus College, Oxford in 1910, then joined the British Museum archaeological team at Carchemish on the Euphrates. In 1914 he worked for the Arab Bureau of army intelligence, then from 1916 fostered and joined the Arab revolt which brought his force to capture Damascus in October 1918. He was an advisor on Arab affairs at the Cairo conference of 1921, and approved of the solution worked out by Churchill; but he became disillusioned by the machinations of the politicians thereafter. He withdrew from his involvement in great affairs in 1922, enlisted in the RAF under the name of John Hume Ross; when his identity was discovered, he switched to the Royal Tank Corps under the name of T E Shaw, returning to the RAF 1925-35. He was killed on his motorcycle, near his cottage on Clouds Hill. His account of his desert campaigns, *Seven pillars of wisdom*, is regarded as a classic.

LINDEMANN, Frederick Alexander ['Prof'] [1886-1957] Scientist. He was born in Baden-Baden, brought up in England but educated in Berlin. PhD 1910. In 1914, in the early days of aviation, he joined the Experimental Physics Station at Farnborough, where he worked out the mathematical theory of aircraft spin, then tested his theory in hazardous experiments. In 1919 he was appointed professor of experimental philosophy (i.e. of physics) at Oxford, and here he built up the Clarendon laboratory to a standard that could compete with Cambridge's Cavendish. FRS 1920. From 1922 he was resident in Christ Church, while being a Fellow of Wadham. He became a friend of Churchill and was from 1940 his scientific adviser, noted not only for his original contributions but for the lucidity with which he could explain abstruse concepts. He was awarded a peerage, becoming Lord Cherwell, in 1941, and advanced to viscount in 1956. PC 1943; CH 1953. He was paymaster-general 1942-45 and 1951-53.

LLOYD GEORGE, David ['The Welsh wizard'] [1863-1945] 1st Earl Lloyd-George of Dwyfor. Prime minister. Brought up by a widowed mother and her brother, a shoemaker, he qualified with honours as a solicitor in 1884. He was elected Liberal MP for Caernarfon Boroughs in 1890, retaining his seat until 1945. He opposed Britain's involvement in the South African war, but championed Welsh causes. President of the Board of Trade 1905; Chancellor of the Exchequer 1908. The House of Lords rejected his 1909 'People's' Budget, but the 1910 election strengthened his reforming hand. Minister of munitions 1915-16, then War minister after death of Kitchener*. Resigned in protest at Asquith's* languid approach to war, succeeded him as Prime Minister in a coalition government December 1916, and brought new urgency to war effort. He and Churchill had been cronies but it was not until 1917 that he offered ministerial rank to his friend. OM 1919. The wartime coalition came apart in 1922 when the Conservatives withdrew; thereafter Lloyd George languished politically; he visited Hitler* in 1936 and flirted with supporting his regime, until he appreciated the true nature of German policies, after which he was critical of Chamberlain's* appeasement. By 1940 he had become too frail to accept Churchill's offer of a post in the War Cabinet, or even the ambassadorship in Washington.

LOW, Sir David (Alexander Cecil) [1891-1963] Cartoonist. Born in Dunedin, New Zealand, and educated as Christchurch Boys' High School, he worked for several New Zealand newspapers and for the Sydney Bulletin before moving to London, where he worked for the *Star*, then from 1927 for the *Evening Standard*. He was critical without being vindictive, and deflated the pompous and pretentious: Colonel Blimp was one of his characters. In 1950 he worked for the *Daily Herald*, and from 1953 for *The Guardian*. He portrayed the Socialist view of Churchill during the 1930s, but his approach was to change dramatically in 1940. Knighted 1962. His celebration of Churchill's 80th birthday is an outstanding piece of cartoon art.

LYTTON, Pamela, Lady [née Plowden] Described by Lady Soames* (in her acclaimed biography of her mother, *Clementine Churchill*) as Churchill's 'first great love', Pamela Plowden was the daughter of the Resident at Hyderabad when Churchill was a subaltern in India. In 1902 she married Victor [Alexander George Robert Bulwer-Lytton] [1876-1947], 2nd Earl of Lytton, who had succeeded his father in the earldom in 1891. The Lyttons and the Churchills became firm friends, with Victor's brother Neville, the painter, as an 'associate' member of the group. Neville would succeed Victor to become the 3rd Earl, while his wife Judith Blunt was the daughter of Wilfrid Scawen Blunt the poet, who was an old friend of Clementine's* mother, Blanche Hozier. The network of friendships and relationships in the Churchills' circle would make a fascinating study in themselves.

M

MacDAVID, Jock [1898- ?] At the age of 18, he was adjutant of Churchill's battalion, the 6th Royal Scots Fusiliers in the Ploegsteert area in 1916, when Churchill abandoned active politics and returned to his original profession of soldiering to serve in France. On one occasion they were together when a shell fragment struck the electric lantern that Churchill was handling, wrecking the battery holder and wounding MacDavid's finger. After a period of sick leave from this injury MacDavid served on the Western Front until August 1918. Martin Gilbert* interviewed him in about 1970; he still recalled the tonic effect Churchill had on the men he commanded.

MACDONALD, (James) Ramsay [1866-1937] British prime minister. Born in Lossiemouth on the Moray Firth in Scotland, MacDonald had little formal education, but became a fervent student of Socialism, joining the Independent Labour Party in 1894. Two years later he married Margaret Ethel Gladstone, daughter of a distinguished scientist; they had six children, of whom five survived into adult life. In 1906 he became MP for Leicester and chairman of his party; five years later he was to be chairman of the Parliamentary Labour group. He resigned this post in 1914, in protest against Britain's becoming involved in war, while conceding that the war must be won; coping with this paradox was beyond his colleagues and he was widely vilified, being defeated in Leicester in 1918; but his courage impressed his party and in 1920 he persuaded both wings of the Labour party to reject Communism. In 1922 he was elected MP for Aberavon division, to become leader of the opposition. Two years later he became briefly prime minister, until the Liberals withdrew their backing of his minority government. In the ensuing election Baldwin's* Tories won an absolute majority and were in power for five years. But the 1929 election gave Labour a narrow majority in the House and MacDonald, now MP for Seaham division, again became prime minister. Shortly the advent of the Depression eroded his support and by 1931 he was the nominal head of an otherwise Tory government and despised by his former Labour colleagues. He resigned as prime minister, and lost his Seaham seat, in 1935, ironically becoming MP for Scottish universities until his death.

MACMILLAN, (Maurice) Harold [1894-1986] Prime minister. Born in London, the grandson of Daniel Macmillan who founded the publishing firm, he was educated at Eton and Balliol College, Oxford, before serving with distinction in the First War. In 1920 he married Lady Dorothy Cavendish, daughter of the 9th Duke of Devonshire. He became an MP in 1924, combining this with his publishing commitments. In the Second War he became Churchill's minister resident in North Africa towards the end of 1942, his sphere of responsibility spreading as countries round the Mediterranean were liberated. As a leading opposition figure, he was effective during Attlee's government, and when Churchill returned to power in 1951 he became minister of housing, fulfilling a pledge to bring the annual figure for houses built up to 300,000. He was next minister of defence 1954-55, then foreign secretary during 1955 and subsequently chancellor of the exchequer, until he succeeded the ailing Eden* in 1957. He was able to mend some of the damage done by the Suez fiasco and seemed to have a magic touch for some years; but by 1963 de Gaulle's veto on admission of UK to the Common Market, and then the Profumo affair (in which his War minister lied about his activities with young women who were also consorting with Russian diplomats) sullied the government's reputation. When Macmillan was laid low by his prostate problems in October 1963, he resigned as prime minister. He had become Chancellor of Oxford University in 1960, was awarded the OM in 1976, and on his 90th birthday in 1984 he became the 1st Earl of Stockton.

MALENKOV, Georgiy Maksimilianovich [1902-88] Russian politician. Born in Orenburg, at the foot of the Urals, he joined the Communist party in 1920, to be involved in the collectivisation of Russian agriculture and Stalin's* purges in the 1930s. He became a Politburo member and deputy prime minister in 1946, and succeeded Stalin as party first secretary and prime minister in 1953. Two years later he resigned, accepting responsibility for the failure of Soviet agricultural policy; he was sent to manage a hydroelectric plant in Kazakhstan, not far from his birthplace.

MARLBOROUGH, 7th Duchess of Marlborough (née Lady Frances Vane-Tempest-Stewart, daughter of the 3rd Marquess of Londonderry) Churchill's paternal grandmother; she and the Blenheim household were taken by surprise by Lady Randolph's* premature labour, a circumstance which she recorded in letters to her co-grandmother Mrs Jerome* in Paris.

MARLBOROUGH, 7th Duke of (John Winston Spencer Churchill) [1822-83] Winston's paternal grandfather. Eton and Oxford. He became MP for Woodstock while Marquess of Blandford, the heir to the dukedom, 1844 and 1847-57, then succeeded to the dukedom. He was lord steward of the household 1866, and lord lieutenant of Ireland 1876-80, his son Lord Randolph Churchill* serving as his secretary during this posting.

MARLBOROUGH, Charles Churchill, 9th Duke of ['Sunny'] [1871-1934] Churchill's cousin and friend. In 1895 he married Consuelo Vanderbilt, an heiress of New York City, whose domineering mother pushed her into marriage regardless of her love for another man; Charles, for his part, tolerated the arrangement for the financial relief it would bring to Blenheim palace. But by 1906 they had separated; she later married Jacques Balsan, Sunny's second wife was Gladys Deacon.[1885-1978].

MARSHALL, Sir Geoffrey KCVO CBE. Physician. He qualified MB BS in 1911, and in 1920 gained his MD and gold medal. He became FRCP in 1928. He was physician to Guy's and the Brompton Hospitals, and was the 'genial but offhand physician' called in by Moran* to advise on the management of Churchill's pneumonia at the beginning of 1943. He was Harveian orator of the Royal College of Physicians, and president of the Thoracic Society.

MOLYNEUX, Sir Richard Frederick [1873-1954] Soldier and courtier. Commissioned into the Blues, he served in the Sudan campaign of 1898 as a lieutenant; he was wounded at Omdurman, being saved by Private Byrne – who was awarded a VC for his bravery – of the 21st Lancers (with which Churchill was then serving). Churchill contributed a piece of skin from his forearm to cover a defect on Molyneux's wound. Molyneux served as a groom-in-waiting to King George V, 1919-36, and was made KCVO in 1935.

MONCRIEFF, Alan Aird CBE. Paediatrician. Middlesex, Hamburg and Paris. MB BS London 1923 (distinction in medicine & surgery and University Medal). MD 1925. FRCP London 1934. Nuffield Professor of Child Health, University of London; paediatrician to Hospital for Sick Children, Great Ormond Street. Author of *Child Health & The State*, 1953.

MONTGOMERY, Bernard Law [1887-1976] 1st Viscount Mongomery of Alamein. Field marshal. St Paul's School, London and Sandhurst. Service in India 1908, Western Front 1914, seriously wounded at 1st Ypres. DSO. Service in Middle East and India between the wars; commanded division in France 1939-40. Commander 8th Army after death of Gott* 1942; victory at Alamein began drive which saw Germans ejected from North Africa. Commanded 21 Army Group 1943, and land forces for invasion of Normandy 1944; committed to handing over command to Eisenhower* after bridgehead secure, but dissension thereafter on matters of tactics; stopped German advance into Ardennes but offended Americans by his hauteur. GCB 1945. Became Chief of Imperial General Staff, viscount, and KG 1946. Deputy supreme commander of NATO (under Eisenhower) 1951; retired 1958. A consummate showman, he inspired the troops who served under him, while antagonising most of his peers.

MOWLEM, (Arthur) Rainsford. Plastic surgeon. Born in Auckland, New Zealand in 1902, he qualified from Otago University in 1924, travelled to London and became FRCS in 1929;

he practised thereafter in Britain, one of four New Zealanders who achieved prominence as pioneers of plastic surgery. He headed departments at the Middlesex Hospital and at Mount Vernon in Northwood, and was plastic surgical consultant to a number of other hospitals in the region. He was president of the British Association of Plastic Surgeons in 1950 and again in 1959. In 1953 he was involved in the management of the burn to Churchill's thumb; on retirement in 1962 he went to live in Malaga, Spain.

N

NEGUS, Sir Victor (Ewings) [1887-1974] Otolaryngologist. He served in the First War, after qualifying MRCS LRCP in 1912; was then house surgeon at the Hospital for diseases of the Throat in Golden Square and took the London MB BS degree in 1921, in which year he also gained his FRCS; his MS (with the University medal) followed in 1924. He was ENT surgeon at King's College Hospital; he was involved in the design of various endoscopes relevant to his field, and the Negus bronchoscope was widely used. In 1930 he was Semon lecturer. He was president of the British Association of Otorhinolaryngologists in 1951, represented his specialty on the Council of the College of Surgeons, and became chairman of the Hunterian Trustees. He saw Churchill about his deafness, as recorded by Moran.

NEWMAN, Philip Harker [1911-94] Orthopaedic surgeon. He qualified in 1934, and became FRCS in 1938. At the outbreak of war he enlisted in the RAMC and, at the time of the Dunkirk evacuation, he was one of those who stayed behind with the wounded and became prisoners of war. In 1942 a safe-conduct for some of the more seriously wounded was arranged but when the party, with Newman as part of the medical escort, was in the middle of France this was revoked. He managed to give the guards the slip, and after a perilous and eventful journey escaped to Spain. He finished the war as a lieutenant-colonel with a DSO and MC. He became orthopaedic surgeon at the Middlesex Hospital, and treated Churchill's hip fracture in 1962. He was president of the British Orthopaedic Association in 1976, in which capacity he hosted the combined meeting of the English-speaking orthopaedic associations, being made CBE that year.

NICOLSON, Sir Harold [1886-1968] Diplomat and writer. Wellington College UK; Balliol College, Oxford. Entered the Foreign Office 1909, his father having been its Permanent Head at the end of a distinguished diplomatic career (indeed Harold was born in the British Legation in Teheran). His own career showed promise, but was ended in 1929 when his wife, the novelist Vita Sackville-West, found the diplomatic round intolerable and he himself became more interested in politics and letters. He wrote biographies of Lord Curzon, and of his own father, Lord Carnock, and entered Parliament in 1935, opposing Chamberlain's* appeasement of the dictators and later serving in Churchill's wartime administration. In 1948 he accepted an invitation to write the official biography of King George V: he produced an acclaimed work, and was made KCVO by his subject's granddaughter.

O

ONASSIS, Aristotle (Socrates) [1906-75] Shipowner. Born in Smyrna [now Izmir] in Turkey, Onassis came as a refugee to Greece at the age of 16. He went to Buenos Aires and made a fortune in tobacco, becoming for a time Greek consul. He bought his first ships in 1932, and built up one of the world's largest independent fleets; he was a pioneer in the building of supertankers. His first marriage was to Athina, daughter of a fellow shipowner, Stavros Livanos; this ended in divorce in 1960. His affair with the singer Maria Callas endured for many years; but in 1968 he married Jackie Kennedy, widow of John F Kennedy the assassinated US president. His yacht *Christina*, on which Churchill family members were regular guests, started life as a corvette of the Royal Canadian Navy.

P

PARRY, Caleb (Hillier) [1755-1822] Physician. The son of a dissenting minister, Joshua Parry (who was Presbyterian minister in Cirencester from 1742). MD Edinburgh 1778. He settled as a physician in Bath, 1779; he was a friend and correspondent of Edward Jenner*, both men recognising the effects of coronary artery disease, and Parry's 1799 text on angina contained material contributed by Jenner and suitably acknowledged. His major work, *The nature, cause, and varieties of the arterial pulse*, was published in 1816.

PATERSON ROSS, Sir James [see ROSS]

PLATT, Sir Harry Bt [1886-1986] Orthopaedic surgeon. A knee infection in childhood led to prolonged disability, yet had two benefits for him: it seeded his interest in orthopaedics, and it turned his attention to music and the arts. Graduating MB BS from London, with the University gold medal, in 1909, he obtained the London MS two years later, and an MD (again with a gold medal) from his native Manchester in 1921. His orthopaedic training was obtained in London and Boston, and he returned to Manchester just before the First War; here he ran a military orthopaedic hospital during the war. He was a founder member of the British Orthopaedic Association, and its president 1934-35, by which time he had a chair in Manchester, one of the first professorial posts in orthopaedics. He was an authority on nerve injuries, on bone grafting, and he developed a valuable procedure for the repair of recurrent dislocation of the shoulder. He served on the Council of the Royal College of Surgeons of England 1940-58, was its first orthopaedic president 1954-57 and, during his term, was able to admit Churchill to the honorary Fellowship he had been awarded in 1943. He remained active, sprightly, and highly articulate up to his death in his 101st year.

R

RAWLINSON, Sir Henry Seymour 2nd Bt, later Baron [1864-1925] Soldier. He was commissioned into the King's Royal Rifles, and served in India and Burma before transferring to the Coldstream Guards in 1891. He then served in the Sudan, in South Africa and as commandant of the Staff College. In 1909 he was promoted major-general and commanded 3 Division. He took over IV Corps in 1914, and it was elements from this corps that took over from Churchill's scratch force at Antwerp. Rawlinson next commanded 1st Army briefly in 1915, 4th Army the following year; and in 1918 he reconstituted 5th Army as 4th, and won several major battles in the second half of 1918. He carried out the evacuation of Allied forces from Russia in 1919 and was made a baron, before becoming commander-in-chief, India from 1920 until his death in Delhi.

RITCHIE, Sir Neil (Methuen) [1897-1983] Soldier. Lancing College, Sandhurst. Commissioned into Black Watch 1914. France and Mesopotamia, DSO MC. Battalion commander, Palestine 1938, France, 1939; Deputy Chief of Staff, Cairo, 1941; appointed to command 8th Army November 1941. Early success not maintained; relieved of command by Auchinleck*, who himself took over, 25 June 1942. Commanded XII Corps in north-west Europe campaign 1944; C-in-Chief Far East Land Forces, Singapore 1947-49; Mission to Washington 1950-51. GBE KCB. Retired to Canada and took up commercial interests. The 'resurrection' of his military career may be attributed to the fact that Auchinleck, who sacked him, was himself sacked shortly after; certainly he did not respond to the criticism of his handling of 8th Army which appeared in Auchinleck's biography.

ROMMEL, Erwin (Johannes Eugen) [1891-1944] German military leader. Born in Heidenheim, he studied in Tubingen, then fought in First War. On the staff of Dresden Military Academy, he was an early Nazi supporter. He commanded Hitler's* headquarters guard at the outbreak of Second

War, and a Panzer division in the 1940 invasion of France. He was given command of the Afrika Corps early in 1941, and established a reputation as an inspired leader in mobile armoured warfare; he also enjoyed a reputation as an honourable foe. Montgomery* was arguably the first to set about puncturing the legend, then defeating Rommel in the Alamein battle of October 1942, and the subsequent pursuit. Rommel came home sick from North Africa, and was one of those in charge of the Normandy defences when he became suspected of involvement in the plot on Hitler's life. He was offered the option of suicide, of which he availed himself.

RÖNTGEN, Wilhelm Conrad [1845-1923] Physicist. He was born in Lennep, then in Prussia, but the family moved to Apeldoorn in the Netherlands after the 1848 revolutions. He studied in Zurich, and subsequently held professorships in Strasbourg (1876-79), Giessen (1879-88) and Würzburg (1888-1900). He became Rector of Würzburg University in 1893; and at this time he was part of a ferment in physics, involving men such as Hertz (who discovered electromagnetic waves in 1888), Kundt and Helmholtz. When these colleagues died in 1894, Röntgen corresponded with Lenard, who had been Hertz's assistant, on the subject of cathode rays. In the course of his experiments during 1895 he became aware of some further and more potent rays – to these he gave the name x-rays, publishing his findings at the end of the year. In 1900 he moved to the chair in Munich, and in 1901 he received the first Nobel prize for physics. From his discovery has developed the whole gamut of medical imaging techniques.

ROOSE, Dr Robson. Medical practitioner. He was the Churchill family's doctor, and in Winston's childhood he was practising in Brighton. When the regime of St George's school, Ascot came to affect Winston's health, he was transferred in 1884 to 'a school in Brighton kept by two ladies'. An attack of pneumonia that year, and another one early in 1886, confirmed the wisdom of the move, and during the second attack Dr Roose spent some days at the boy's bedside. Roose was also involved in the medical care of Lord Randolph, and corresponded with Dr Buzzard* on the matter.

ROOSEVELT, Franklin Delano [1882-1945] The 32nd American president. Born into a patrician family in Hyde Park, NY, he qualified as a lawyer in 1907, and was a New York state senator 1910-13. He was assistant secretary of the Navy 1913-20. In 1920 he was Democratic candidate for the vice-presidency, but the following year he contracted poliomyelitis and suffered widespread paralysis of both legs. In spite of this disability he served as Governor of New York 1928-32, then became president. He attacked his country's economic crisis by his 'New Deal', and was re-elected in 1936 and 1940. He strove to keep the US out of the war, while agreeing with Churchill on the provision of war supplies and munitions (at a price!): this somewhat anomalous position was resolved when Japan attacked Pearl Harbor and, four days later, Germany declared war on the U S. Roosevelt was elected president again in 1944, but he was a sick man when the three Allied leaders met at Yalta early in 1945, and his paranoia about British imperialism led him to pander to Stalin's* demands in a way that laid the foundations for the Cold War. He died soon after; and his country determined that future presidents would be eligible only for two terms.

ROSS, Sir James Paterson [1895-1980] Surgeon. He was the pupil of Harvey Cushing and private assistant to Lord Moynihan; he joined the professorial surgical unit at Bart's, and succeeded George Gask in 1935. The two of them published a pioneering work on the sympathetic nervous system. In June 1947 he and Sir Thomas Dunhill* were involved in performing a hernia repair operation on Churchill (their respective roles are the subject of speculation); and in 1948 he and Sir James Learmonth of Edinburgh performed a lumbar sympathectomy on King George VI, whose leg was in jeopardy from arterial disease. Both men were made KCVO (which implies parity!) In 1957 he became president of the Royal College of Surgeons of England, in succession to Sir Harry Platt*; he had, during the 1930s, been a Hunterian professor of the College on three occasions – an achievement which has been matched but not, so far as I am aware, bettered.

S

SCADDING, John Guyett [1907-99] Chest physician. MB BS London 1930. MD (University Medal) 1932. MRCP 1932, FRCP 1941. A Middlesex graduate, he spent much of the Second War in command of the medical division of 19 General Hospital, RAMC, at Fayid in the Canal Zone, in the rank of Lt-Col. With his colleague and former chief Evan Bedford* he was called to see Churchill in December 1943 at Carthage, when an episode of pneumonia was complicated by the development of atrial fibrillation. He practised at the Brompton Hospital for Chest Diseases (to which he had been appointed in 1939), was Dean of the Institute for Diseases of the Chest, and professor of medicine in the Postgraduate Medical School. He was a vice-president of the Royal College of Physicians of London, its Bradshaw lecturer in 1949 and Lumleian lecturer in 1973; a founder and subsequent president of the Thoracic Society and first editor of the journal *Thorax*; and consultant in diseases of the chest to the Army. In his retirement he lived in Beaconsfield, from where he wrote a charming BMA paper in 1993, on his 'summons to Carthage'.

SEAGO, Edward Brian [1910-74] Painter. A heart complaint curtailed his formal education from the age of 14, but he studied painting under Bertram Priestman RA and had his first London exhibition in 1929. In the Second War he became a camouflage officer, and designed the insignia of the Airborne forces. After being invalided out of the army in 1944 he accepted Alexander's* invitation to paint scenes of the Italian campaign; these paintings were exhibited in London in 1945 and later formed the basis of a book. Although primarily a landscape artist he painted portraits of King George VI and of the present Queen.

SEDDON, Sir Herbert (John) [1903-77] Orthopaedic surgeon. Born in Derby, educated Manchester, Oxford and St Bartholomew's. MRCS LRCP 1925; MB BS London [Gold medal] 1928. FRCS 1928. MA DM [Oxon] 1940. CMG. Knighted 1964. Ann Arbor, Michigan as Instructor in Surgery 1930. Royal National Orthopaedic Hospital 1932. Professor of Orthopaedic Surgery, Oxford 1940. Investigated peripheral nerve injuries and wrote authoritative text. Set up treatment centres Malta and Mauritius following polio outbreaks 1943. Director of Studies, Institute of Orthopaedics, Royal National Orthopaedic Hospital 1948-65, professor 1965-67; he elucidated the pathology of tuberculous paraplegia, and made the hospital into a centre of international repute. President British Orthopaedic Association 1960-61. Called to see Churchill in consultation after his 1960 stroke.

SEELY, John (Edward Bernard) [Jack] [1868-1947] Politician; friend of Churchill. Harrow and Trinity College, Cambridge. Served in South Africa, DSO 1900. Tory MP for Isle of Wight 1900-06; but resigned from Conservative party 1904. Became Liberal MP for Abercromby division, Liverpool 1906-10, Ilkeston division, Derbyshire 1910-22 and Isle of Wight 1923-24. Secretary of state for War 1912-14; criticised for role in Curragh incident. Commanded a Canadian brigade in France 1914-18. He received a barony in 1933, becoming Lord Mottistone.

SEMON, Sir Felix [1849-1921] Laryngologist. Born in Danzig of Prussian Jewish parentage; MD Berlin. He came to London in 1874, and became physician in charge of the throat department of St Thomas's Hospital 1882-97, and laryngologist to what was then the National Hospital for the Paralysed and Epileptic 1887-1909. He practised in the period when the throat physicians, who also dealt with diseases of the nose and chest, were on the verge of merging with the ear surgeons (otologists) to produce the specialty of ear, nose and throat (ENT) surgery. Semon became FRCP in 1885, was knighted in 1897 and naturalised in 1901. In 1905 he became KCVO. He is commemorated in the Semon lecture, one of which was given by Sir Victor Negus*.

SNEYD-KYNNERSLEY, H W. See Kynnersley, H W Sneyd.

SOAMES, Mary [née Churchill, b.1922] The youngest Churchill daughter, she joined the ATS in 1941 and served in anti-aircraft batteries in England and north-west Europe, and also as her father's ADC on overseas journeys. MBE 1945. In 1947 she married Captain Christopher (later Lord) Soames, who became her father's right-hand man in the management of Chartwell, and a minister in Macmillan's* government; he later became a successful diplomat. Theirs was the durable Churchill marriage of their generation. Lady Soames was made DBE in 1980, and a Lady of the Garter in 2002. She has been an honorary Fellow of Churchill College since 1983, and a strong supporter of its Archives Centre. She has written the definitive biography of her mother, and has followed this with her own reminiscences.

STALIN, Josef (Iosif Vissarionivich Dzugashvili) [1879-1953] Russian dictator. Born in Gori in Georgia, the son of a drunkard cobbler, he grew up in poverty but obtained some schooling and then entered the Tiflis Orthodox Seminary in Tbilisi, only to be expelled in 1899, probably for advocating Marxism. In the decade 1902-13 he was an active revolutionary, arrested, imprisoned, and twice exiled to Siberia. He played an active part in the October Revolution of 1917, becoming a member of the Politburo. In 1922 he became general secretary to the Party Central Committee, and built the power base that enabled him to succeed Lenin in 1924. He assumed the name 'Stalin' – man of steel. He reorganised the Soviet economy with a disastrous policy of 'collectivisation', and his measures against those who opposed him are considered to have led to the deaths of 10 million people. In the period 1934-38 he purged the Party, government, armed forces and academia, so depriving his country of much of its capabilities. He formed an alliance with Hitler*, but this did not prevent the German invasion of June 1941. He demanded the opening of a 'second front' to ease pressure on his forces, while working towards the absorption of Eastern Europe into the Soviet sphere. By his duping of the ailing Roosevelt* he assured the situation that became the Cold War. He died in 1953; subsequent Russian opinion has come to blame him for everything that went wrong in the Soviet era; he has become a convenient figure behind whom his people can shelter to claim absolution.

STANLEY, Venetia [1887-1948] She was the friend of Violet Asquith* and a cousin of Clementine Churchill*; she and Violet exchanged catty letters about Clementine upon her engagement to Winston, though all three women would become more genuine friends over time. Because of her friendship with Violet, Venetia was much in the company of Violet's father, Herbert Asquith* the prime minister, who became infatuated with her, and took to writing indiscreet letters to her, even during Cabinet meetings. When in mid-1915 she blandly informed him that she was engaged to marry Edwin Montagu, one of his junior colleagues, he was devastated.

STURDEE, Jo (later Countess of Onslow) In 1942 she became a member of Churchill's secretarial team; she wrote no letters home and kept no diary during the war, but from 1946 she relaxed this rule, and her letters to her family describe the pattern of the 1946 American tour and a visit to Marrakech at the end of 1947.

SUTHERLAND, Graham Vivian [1903-80] Painter and printmaker. Epsom College and Goldsmith's College School of Art. Taught engraving at Chelsea School of Art 1926. Turned to painting after visit to Pembrokeshire 1934. Commissioned to produce giant tapestry, *Christ in glory*, for Coventry cathedral 1952, completed 1962. First portrait was of Somerset Maugham in 1949; arguably his worst that of Churchill, for presentation by both Houses of Parliament 1954, for his subject's 80th birthday – Churchill hated it, and Clementine had it destroyed. Trustee of Tate gallery 1948, resigned 1954 after disagreement with other trustees. OM 1960

T

TITO, Josip Broz, Marshal [1892-1980] Yugoslav leader. The son of a Croatian locksmith, he served in the Austro-Hungarian army in the First War, was taken prisoner by the Russians, and joined the Red Army after the Revolution. On his return to Yugoslavia he helped form the local Communist party and named himself 'Tito'. He was imprisoned 1928-34; on his release he moved round Europe seeking support for his party, then took part in the Spanish Civil War. He returned home in 1939, and after the German invasion of his country he became a partisan leader. He found himself at cross purposes with the royalist Mihailovic, who was then the 'preferred' resistance leader; but a British mission led by Fitzroy Maclean formed the view that Tito had more to offer, and thereafter it was to him that Allied support was given. After the Germans were expelled Tito executed Mihailovic, got rid of the monarchy and established a Communist state; but it was a state that thought for itself and did not become a mere Soviet appendage. After his death, Yugoslavia imploded.

TREVES, Sir Frederick Bt [1853-1923] Surgeon. He was a student at the London Hospital 1871-75, joining the surgical staff of the hospital (now the Royal London) in 1879. He demonstrated anatomy and built up a considerable reputation as surgeon and teacher alike. In an era when the two developments – anaesthesia and asepsis – had made safe abdominal surgery a reality, he was a leading figure. He became surgeon-extraordinary to Queen Victoria in 1900, the year in which he spent some time in South Africa as a surgeon with the Natal Field Force. In 1901 he was made KCVO and in 1902, when he dealt with King Edward VII's appendix abscess, he became a baronet and serjeant-surgeon to the King. He died in retirement at Vevey.

W

WAVELL, Archibald Percival, 1st Earl Wavell [1883-1950] Soldier and man of letters. Winchester and Sandhurst. Commissioned into the Black Watch. India 1903-10. Attached to Russian army 1911-12, and liaison with Grand Duke Nicholas's army in Turkey 1916. Palestine 1917-20; 1937-38. Formed Middle East Command July 1939; cleared Italians out of Cyrenaica and shortly north-east Africa, 1940-1; then obliged to send troops into Greece and Crete, with resulting loss of recent North African gains, 1941. Commander-in-chief India 1941, supreme commander, South-West Pacific, December 1941-43. Viceroy of India 1943-47, working patiently towards a settlement of the independence issue. GCB 1941; GCSI GCIE PC, viscount and field marshal 1943. Earl 1947. His poetry anthology, *Other men's flowers*, is outstanding for his commentary as much as for its content.

WEBB-JOHNSON, Alfred Edward, Baron [1880-1958] Born Alfred Edward Johnson in Stoke-on-Trent, he incorporated his mother's maiden surname into his own name as a tribute to her influence on him. Newcastle-under-Lyme High School, Owens College, Manchester. MB ChB 1903, FRCS 1906. He came to the Middlesex Hospital in 1908, where Bland-Sutton became his mentor and friend. Served throughout First War, as surgeon in 14 General Hospital and later its CO, then consultant surgeon, Boulogne area. DSO 1916, CBE 1919. Dean of the Middlesex Hospital medical school 1919-25; chairman of planning committee for new hospital, opened 1935. Surgeon to Queen Mary 1936-53. President of the Royal College of Surgeons of England 1941-49; 'drove' the rebuilding and expansion of the College after severe bomb damage in 1941. Baronet 1945, baron 1948, GCVO 1954.

WILSON, Charles McMoran, 1st Lord Moran [1882-1977] Physician. Pocklington Grammar School, St Mary's Hospital. MB BS 1908; MD 1913. Medical officer on Western Front 1914-16; MC 1916. Assistant physician, St Mary's 1919; dean of medical school 1920. Knighted 1938. Invited by Cabinet to become Churchill's personal physician, 1940. President of the Royal

College of Physicians of London 1941-50. Baron 1943. Published *The anatomy of courage* (1945), *Winston Churchill: the struggle for survival* (1966).

WILSON, Henry Maitland, 1st Baron ['Jumbo'] [1881-1964] Soldier. Eton and Sandhurst. Commissioned into the Rifle Brigade 1900, in time to serve in South Africa. India 1907. Staff appointments 1914-18. DSO 1917. North-West frontier, India; instructor at Staff College. GOC-in-C, British troops, Egypt 1939; GOC, British Forces in Palestine and Transjordan 1941; GOC-in-C 9th Army, C-in-C Middle East 1943; Supreme commander Mediterranean and field marshal, 1944. Joint Staff Mission in Washington 1945-47. GBE 1941; GCB 1944, baron 1946. President of Old Etonian association 1948-49.

Y

YEOMAN, Philip Metcalfe. [1923-1997] Orthopaedic surgeon. Emmanuel College & University College Hospital. As a medical student went with a relief team to the Belsen concentration camp. MB BChir [Cantab] 1947, MA 1948. FRCS 1957. MD, awarded for research on brachial plexus lesions. After posts in Leeds, Cambridge and London practised in Bath from 1964. Saw Churchill with Professor Seddon* following 1960 stroke; assisted at operation for hip fracture 1962. ABC Travelling Fellow to North America 1964. Vice-president British Orthopaedic Association 1985 [Robert Jones Gold Medal 1963]; Council RCS 1984-92.

NOTE ON THE ILLUSTRATIONS

Few people of his time can have been more photographed or otherwise depicted than Winston Churchill, so that images of him are as easy to accumulate as they are difficult to identify precisely. For that reason I have found the proper attribution of items in my own collection quite challenging; and I could not have managed without the expert assistance, patience and kindness of the Director of the Churchill Archives Centre, Mr Allen Packwood, and his colleague Mr Philip Cosgrove. Thanks to them I have been able for the most part to learn where to turn and whom to approach, in order to obtain copyright clearance. To any persons whose copyright may unwittingly have been infringed, I offer my sincere apologies, my assurance that Messrs Packwood and Cosgrove are entirely blameless, and my hope that those copyright holders will be pleased to see their material used in such a good cause as the evaluation of Sir Winston's medical history.

From the resources of the Churchill Archives Centre itself I would like to acknowledge the following:
Fig. 1:   Lord Randolph & Jenny Jerome as an engaged couple: CHAR 28 041 046
Fig. 9:   WSC revisits the armoured train: CHPH 18 8
Fig.10:   WSC and Clementine as an engaged couple CHPH 1A F1 006
Fig. 18: WSC leaving hospital, 1931 CHPH 1A/F2/25
Fig. 20: WSC convalescent after paratyphoid, 1932 CHPH 1A/F2/25a
Fig. 28: Big 3 at Yalta CHPH 1A/F3/40c
Fig. 35: Treeplanting at Churchill College CCPH 4/2
Fig. 39: Cranes dip in salute CHPH 73
Fig. 43: WSC's wedding outfit CSCT 5/3
And to the Master and Fellows of Churchill College I am grateful for permission to use the photographs of WSC as First Lord [fig.11], and the Churchill College copy of the Orpen portrait of WSC [fig. 48].

The Imperial War Museums have been kind enough to permit the reproduction of the following:
Fig. 21: WSC broadcasting on VE Day H41846
Fig. 26: WSC convalescent at Carthage, Christmas 1943 NA10074
Fig. 45: The V sign A17610
The image [fig. 42b] of WSC in dark suit, with bow tie, watch chain, and striped trousers, appears as Fig. 9 in Best's biography, and is there attributed to IWM, who cannot locate it but are unconcerned at its use here.

Messrs Curtis Brown, as custodians of the © Broadwater collection, have authorised the use of the following:
Fig. 3:   WSC as a Harrow schoolboy
Fig. 8:   WSC playing polo, using a splint to protect his unstable right shoulder
Fig. 12: The camel trip to the Pyramids, 1921
Fig. 15a: Arrival at Dundee for Armistice Day service, 1922
They have also validated my use of the letters bearing WSC's signature, which form fig. 38.

The Bone and Joint Journal has granted permission to use the following images from early issues of the British Volume of *The Journal of Bone and Joint Surgery*:
Fig. 5:   Brockbank W, Griffiths DL: Orthopaedic surgery in the 16-17th centuries.
          J Bone Joint Surg [Br] 1948; 30B: 365; fig. 2

Fig. 6:   Osmond-Clarke H: Habitual dislocation of the shoulder. 30B: 19; fig.1
          Adams, JC: Recurrent dislocation of the shoulder. 30B: 26; figs.7, 9
Fig. 7a: In memoriam: A S Blundell Bankart 1951; 33B: 278.
Fig. 37: Philip Newman: 1977; 59B: 106.

The use of the Karsh portrait deserves a word of explanation. In order to discuss the mechanics of the injury I was anxious to illustrate the position of the scar that resulted from WSC's 1931 encounter with a car in New York, and I had noticed that the edge-lit Karsh image showed this scar better than many other photographs. My request to use a detail (centred on the scar and including one eye and some forehead) as fig. 19 reached Julie Grahame, who deals with such matters. Not unreasonably she felt that such a detail – though ideal for my purposes – did not do justice to the splendour of the whole portrait; and she therefore laid down the condition that the portrait itself should also be published. Of the various ways this might be done, she was imaginative enough to fall in with my suggestion of using it for the frontispiece, rather than say putting it, small scale, alongside the detail. Given the qualities of the defiant pose that made the Karsh portrait so admired in 1941, and Churchill's refusal to be daunted by a multitude of often life-threatening medical conditions, such a frontispiece is ideal for this present work. It is a delight, therefore, to acknowledge the kind permission of © the estate of Yousuf Karsh to employ the Karsh portrait as frontispiece, and the detail as fig. 19.

For specific permissions, I am indebted to other helpful friends and colleagues:
    - to Professor Sam Mellick, for the illustration of Washington Cathedral and the plaque
      there which records Churchill's speech of December 1941 [fig. 22]
    - to Peter Fabian, for the photograph of WSC arriving for a Garter ceremony [fig. 35] and
      the series of photographs of WSC at the electorate gala [fig. 36]
    - to Professor Timothy Briggs, for the x-ray of WSC's hip fracture, [fig. 37a]
    - to Brett Newell, for securing the agreement of his friends the Pol-Rogers to the use of
      the illustration of WSC and Odette Pol-Roger [fig. 41]
    - to Harriet Bowes-Lyon, who has once again allowed me to use a detail from the group
      photograph of her father's farewell from No.10 in 1941 [fig. 44b]

The Royal Colleges have been most cooperative:
    - the Royal College of Physicians of London, in allowing the use of the Annigoni portrait
      of Lord Moran as PRCP [fig. 46] ;
    - the Royal College of Surgeons of England, for the following:
      the photographs of Sir Harry Platt [fig. 7b]; of Sir Winston's visit to the College to sign
      the roll of Fellows [fig. 24]; of Harold Edwards [fig. 29]; of Sir James Paterson Ross [fig.
      31b]; of Lord Brain and Sir Victor Negus [fig. 32].
      The College also directed me to an image of Sir Crisp English [fig. 14] on the website
      of the Sudbury Museum in Suffolk; my request to Sudbury for clearance went
      unanswered, and I have taken silence for assent.
    - the Royal Australasian College of Surgeons, for the portrait of Sir Thomas Dunhill [fig.
      31a] – though I see that I hold the copyright for this reproduction, having described the
      Dunhill portrait and its subject in my *Portraits* book in 1993.

Over the years I have been accumulating, jackdaw fashion, an extensive collection of Churchill-related images. The photograph of the ship *Empress of Australia* [fig. 17] is enlarged from a cigarette card I collected as a small boy (during Churchill's 'Locust years' and long before I knew of the Churchill Troupe). Others lack a 'normal' provenance, such as the photograph of WSC as a young man with an incredibly fashionable collar [fig. 42a] which appeared, quite without attribution, in a flier for an edition of the *Dictionary of National Biography*. The drawing of Lord Randolph as Chancellor of the Exchequer [fig. 2] was used by his son in his biography *My early Life*, but its source in unrecorded. My own photographs, from Zurich [fig. 30] and my time at Churchill College – the statue [fig.28b] and the ceremonial oak tree dwarfing Allen Packwood [fig. 35b] – are straightforward enough; but in several instances I am at a loss to determine the ultimate sources of particular items – the photograph of Budget Day 1924 [fig. 16], for instance. Nor can I identify the source of two Dundee images from 1922 [fig. 15b,c], but they are important in depicting the extent to which Churchill was unwell after his appendicectomy operation. This confusion has made it difficult to be sure of attributions.

The Low cartoon, done for Churchill's 80th birthday, was one of my earliest pictorial acquisitions of Churchilliana. Published in a long defunct newspaper in New Zealand, it was carefully folded away into a book, *Aspects of British Art*, published by Collins in 1947, in which the chapter on *British Cartoonists, Caricaturists and Comic Artists* was contributed by David Low himself. Here it fitted in at the page where Low had reproduced, in colour, one of his own cartoons, 'The Past meets the Present: Jubilee day on Olympus'. Its descriptive caption is worth quoting:

> The gathering includes such well-known gods as Ramsay MacDonald, George Bernard Shaw, Wells, Maxton, Reith, Beaverbrook, Lloyd George, Barrie, Churchill and C B Cochran: also, some obscure – and perhaps legendary – young men.

On the left, the young men are gesticulating vigorously across the surface of the Olympian cloud towards a gathering of middle-aged (and except for Shaw, no longer gesturing) counterparts. Many of the characters there appear also in this narrative of mine; and I am impressed particularly by the affection for his subjects that Low displays.

This same kindliness shone through his cartoon of a benevolent and white-spatted Churchill (done in the 1920s and affectionately labelled 'Winston') which graced the cover of the Pan Books paperback of Philip Guedalla's *Mr Churchill*, which its author subtitled 'A Portrait'.

And equally it shines through the 80th birthday cartoon, slightly creased and faded though this may be. A cartoonist must often criticise or lampoon his subject; a great cartoonist can do so without resorting to meanness, For that reason (being unable to trace its present copyright owner, if any) I have dared to feel that my fellow New Zealander would not object to its publication in a work of this sort. I have therefore taken the liberty of scanning my newspaper original to form fig. 34.

I have taken a comparable liberty with a detail from the illustration facing page 782 of my copy of the Moran diaries, of Lord Moran delivering a bulletin to newsmen outside the Churchill residence at 28 Hyde Park Gate. The illustration is credited to Thomson Newspapers, but I have been unable to trace their successors, and it is desirable that Lord Moran's role as a medical herald should be depicted as fig. 47.

And in assembling small representations of three men who were summoned to Carthage by Lord Moran in December 1943 – Brig D E Bedford, Lt-Col J G Scadding and Lt-Col G A H Buttle – and were there able, between them, to restore Churchill's health and Harold Macmillan's equanimity, I have 'borrowed' an image passed to me by Dr Ronald Easthope, one credited to Nick Sinclair in a BMJ obituary, and a detail from a group of senior medical officers photographed in September 1942 by Col R D King. I feel that the value of having this expert group reassembled after so long deserves to excuse the irregularity of the process that resulted in fig. 25.

The photographs of Freyberg showing Fraser round the ruins of Cassino, and of Churchill and Freyberg deep in discussion in the desert [figs. 27a, 40] are included by courtesy of the

Alexander Turnbull library; and the other 'desert' picture of Churchill [fig. 23] was given to me, not long before he died, by Sir John White, who had treasured it since he took the photograph in August 1942, only to find that the censor embargoed it. For this reason it did not enter Sir John's 'official' collection, which is central to New Zealand's record of its military engagement in the Mediterranean theatre. It is possible, in retrospect, to feel some sympathy for the censor, who did not wish to release an image that might be construed as indicating a grim pessimism in the PM, especially in a year of reverses and just two months after the embarrassing occasion when, visiting Roosevelt, Churchill had to accept, in the presence of his host, the news of the surrender of Tobruk.

The signed photograph of Churchill that Peter Fraser brought back in 1944 [fig. 27b] is reproduced by permission of the New Zealand Parliamentary Collection, in which it is SA 972; and the portrait of Churchill by Marcus King which appears on the dust jacket is SA 15 in that collection.

To create the diagram [fig. 33] of the layout of the brain, I worked from a drawing by the late Professor R J Last, who taught me to appreciate anatomy, at the English College in 1955. He illustrated his teaching with brilliant diagrams and, in the original edition of his text book, published in 1954, he transferred these to the page. I valued my friendship with Ray Last, then and later, and the devising of fig. 33 was an opportunity to pay tribute to a valued mentor.

The letters signed by WSC during his convalescence in 1962-63 [fig. 38] were made available to me by Mr Anthony Woodhead, who was my host when I spoke to the Epping-Woodford branch of the Churchill Centre in 2010. And the photograph of me, standing outside the front door of Chartwell, was taken by Mr Nigel Guest, my host in 2012 when I spoke there.

INDEX